VOLUME 18   NUMBER 4   OCTOBER 2006

Editors' Introduction   471

SETTING IN MOTION
Curated and edited by Susan Jahoda and Jesal Kapadia   476

  Pasolini Pa* Palestine
  Ayreen Anastas   478

  The Quick and the Dead
  Stephen Andrews   480

  Three Poems for *Rethinking Marxism* 2006
  Gregg Bordowitz   482

  PLAY
  Moyra Davey   486

  I Won't Drown On That Levee and You Ain't Gonna
  Break My Back
  Ashley Hunt   488

  ... of a worm in a pomegranate
  Susan Jahoda   500

  This is not a ...
  Jesal Kapadia   502

  Departure
  Lin + Lam   504

  Love/Torture
  Ulrike Müller   506

  Possible Models
  Jenny Perlin   508

  POW
  Emily Roysdon   510

Vera
Jason Simon   512

Talking oneself out of a corner out of the corner
of one's mouth
Julia Meltzer and David Thorne   514

Hospitality
James Pei-Mun Tsang   516

Architecture, New Orleans and the Specter
of Ecological Justice
Yates Mckee   518

ART/ICULATIONS
From Imperialism to Transnational Capitalism:
The Venice Biennial as a "Transitional Conjuncture"
Yahya M. Madra   525

Capital: At Least It Kills Time
A. Kiarina Kordela   539

REMARX
Interests and the Political Terrain of Time
Geoff Mann   565

Marx's Learning Process: Against Correcting Marx
with Hegel
Wolfgang Fritz Haug   572
Translated by Eric Canepa

REVIEWS
*Fragments of Development: Nation, Gender, and
the Space of Modernity,* by Suzanne Bergeron
Chizu Sato   585

*Just Around the Corner: The Paradox of the Jobless
Recovery,* by Stanley Aronowitz
Richard D. Wolff   589

Imaginary States: Studies in Cultural Transnationalism,
by Peter Hitchcock
Maria Markantonatou   590

Notes on Contributors   593

RETHINKING MARXISM

Subscription Information

RETHINKING MARXISM is a peer-reviewed journal published quarterly (January, April, July and October), by Routledge Journals, an imprint of Taylor & Francis, 4 Park Square, Milton Park, Abingdon, Oxfordshire OX14 4RN, UK.

Annual Subscription, Volume 18, 2006 (Print ISSN 0893-5696)

Institutional US$315   £189   Individual US$79   £46   Student Rate US$26   £16
Online only US$299   £180 (plus tax where applicable)

An institutional subscription to the print edition includes free access for any number of concurrent users across a local area network to the online edition, ISSN 1475-8059.
For more information, visit our website: http://www.tandf.co.uk/journals
For a complete and up-to-date guide to Taylor & Francis journals and books publishing programmes, and details of advertising in our journals, visit our website:
http://www.tandf.co.uk/journals

Dollar rates apply to subscribers in all countries except the UK and the Republic of Ireland where the pound sterling price applies. All subscriptions are payable in advance and all rates include postage. Journals are sent by air to the USA, Canada, Mexico, India, Japan and Australasia. Subscriptions are entered on an annual basis, i.e. January to December. Payment may be made by sterling cheque, dollar cheque, international money order, National Giro, or credit card (Amex, Visa, Mastercard).

Ordering Information
USA/Canada: Taylor & Francis Inc., Journals Department, 325 Chestnut Street, 8th Floor, Philadelphia, PA 19106, USA. **Europe/Rest of World:** T & F Customer Services, T & F Informa UK Ltd, Sheepen Place, Colchester, Essex CO3 3LP, UK. Tel: +44 (0)207 017 5544; Fax: +44 (0)207 017 5198; Email:tf.enquiries@tfinforma.com.

Advertising Enquiries
USA/Canada: The Advertising Manager, Taylor & Francis Inc., 325 Chestnut Street, 8th Floor, Philadelphia, PA 19106, USA. Tel: +1 (215) 625 8900. Fax: +1 (215) 625 2240. **EU/RoW:** The Advertising Manager, Taylor & Francis, 4 Park Square, Milton Park, Abingdon, Oxfordshire OX14 4RN, UK. Tel: +44 (0)207 017 6000. Fax: +44 (0)207 017 6336.

The print edition of this journal is typeset by Datapage, Dublin, Ireland and printed on ANSI conforming acid free paper by Bell & Bain Ltd, Glasgow, UK. The online edition of this journal is hosted by MetaPress at http://www.journalsonline.tandf.co.uk

Disclaimer. The Society (Association for Economic and Social Analysis) and Taylor & Francis make every effort to ensure the accuracy of all the information (the "Content") contained in its publications. However, the Society and Taylor & Francis and its agents and licensors make no representations or warranties whatsoever as to the accuracy, completeness or suitability for any purpose of the Content and disclaim all such representations and warranties whether express or implied to the maximum extent permitted by law. Any views expressed in this publication are the views of the authors and are not the views of the Society and Taylor & Francis.

Abstracting and Indexing Service. RETHINKING MARXISM is currently indexed in *Alternative Press Index, International Bibliography of the Social Sciences, Connexions Digest, L'Autre Amerique, Film Literature Index,* and *Left Index.* Abstracts are published by *Human Resources Abstracts, Sage Publishing Administration Abstracts,* and *Sociological Abstracts.*

Editors' Introduction

In this issue

as part of the run-up to the Rethinking Marxism 2006 conference to be held at the University of Massachusetts Amherst, we devote a special section to "Setting in Motion," the art exhibit curated by Susan Jahoda and Jesal Kapadia for RM06. The exhibit itself will set in motion a provocative variety of individual and collaborative projects from across the United States and around the world, utilizing a wide range of media—including film, animation, video, and texts. The goal, drawing on the recent work of Jacques Rancière, is not to occupy the space created by the apparent weakening of "real" politics—not to substitute art for politics—but to relocate, redefine, and reshape that space. Here, using capsule summaries and a selection of poetry, stills, and images from fourteen distinct projects, Jahoda and Kapadia undertake to represent on the printed page how the works in the exhibit enact new ways of sensing and sense-making, of combining heterogeneous elements and different politics of sensibility, of making visible what has been rendered invisible, allowing new objects and new subjects to appear, disclosing hidden possibilities—in short, how they become "critical art" by creating and sustaining scenes of conflict, collision, and dissensus.

Yahya M. Madra, in his contribution to the art/iculations series, also confronts the issues surrounding the political aesthetics of contemporary critical art. Utilizing the Marxian critique of political economy in a subtle and creative manner, Madra contextualizes and interrogates the latest in the long series of Venice Biennials (the Venice Biennial being one among a burgeoning number of art biennials worldwide). Given the current penchant for combining national exhibition halls and curated multinational exhibits, Madra locates the Venice and other such international biennials within a "transitional conjuncture" in the mode of appropriating art: from art as a "sublimated object that functions as the representative of the national identity" to a new institutional form, one that seeks to combine the contradictory tendencies of, on the one hand, radicalized and pluralized art practices and, on the other hand, transnational corporate funding. What roles do these proliferating art biennials play? In Madra's view, they impose and create transnational aesthetic standards; they have become the new art market, in which the practices of selected artists are valorized; and they are part of the "festivalization of the arts" conducted and coordinated by global-city governments, transnational corporations, and internationally renowned curators. What then of the "critical art" that is exhibited in these biennials, which seeks to resist the commodity form by offering strong political perspectives and by assuming forms (such as performances and installations) that are difficult to market? The problem is that much of the art Madra encountered in Venice

ISSN 0893-5696 print/1475-8059 online/06/040471-04
© 2006 Association for Economic and Social Analysis
DOI: 10.1080/08935690600901178

Routledge
Taylor & Francis Group

was often formulaic, sterile, and "reformist"—"not only *despite* but *because* of the political nature" of the works. As he explains, the art works were reformist to the extent that they represented an acceptance of, and then an attempt to navigate within, the formal structure of the biennial. The alternative outlined by Madra is to extend the questioning of the "material and institutional conditions of the imperial/national mode of appropriation of art" (by, for example, Hans Haacke in 1993 and Daniel Knorr in 2005) to critically engage the "new transnational mode of appropriating art qua spectacle."

A. Kiarina Kordela's goal in "Capital: At Least It Kills Time" is to formulate a theory of temporality and historicity appropriate to secular capitalist modernity. She then uses this theory to enter into a critical dialogue with several thinkers whose work plays an important role in redefining contemporary Marxist thought. Kordela is concerned, in particular, with theories of capitalist stage development (as utilized, for example, by Fredric Jameson), the so-called Neo-Spinozist Left (associated, in different ways, with both Antonio Negri and Michael Hardt and Gilles Deleuze and Félix Guattari), and deconstruction (especially Jacques Derrida). What is at stake, for Kordela, is a conception of history as a set of "synchronic blocks," each with its own formal logic, that makes it possible to understand the formal conditions of the existing block that need to be changed and to move to a "really other historical block." The key concepts Kordela deploys come from Marx and Lacan, who in her view shared the goal of carrying out a "transcendental critique" of value (both economic and linguistic), and Spinoza, who conceptualized the transcendent as both cause and effect of the historical. The resulting "pantheism of value" *is* the synchronic temporality of capital, and the emergence of a different historical block—in the here and now and not in some diachronic future—depends not on objective knowledge but, in Lacanian terms, on "surplus-enjoyment." The problem with Jameson's stages theory is that it adjoins the fantasmic surplus to objective knowledge (involving either the perpetuation of capitalism or its inevitable collapse). As for the "Neo-Spinozists," they either collapse the object of desire and the time of capital or construct desire as the necessary endpoint of some diachronic trajectory. Finally, for the deconstructionist left, there is no otherness, since the future is eternally deferred. For Kordela it is important to understand that capital has already killed the linear sequence of time, and that the "so-called 'future' is another present, yet unrealized block whose structure can be articulated only through its formal difference from the given past and present blocks."

The first essay in the Remarx section also focuses on the issue of time and history—in this case, to confront the problem of white working-class conservatism in the United States—but with an approach quite different from that of Kordela. Like Kordela, Geoff Mann argues that it is important to take the "temporal orientation" of politics seriously. However, he wants to distinguish the anti-futural "interest" articulated in and by the conservative, proto-fascist politics of the Bush regime with an "interest in the future" heralded by the Left. This, by way of moving beyond the given (Weberian or other) interests often imputed to the working class, and the resulting false-consciousness analysis (of writers like Thomas Frank), in order to explain "what makes capitalism so bearable, even welcome, despite its 'unbearability'?" Mann believes it is important to recognize that interests are neither natural nor universal, not grounded in some set of underlying needs or psychic processes. His own suggestion is that interests "represent, or are a product of, a struggle-search for political subjectivity or agency" that is necessarily oriented toward the future even when it is haunted by the past. The challenge for critical intellectuals is to help radicalize this struggle-search, by acknowledging and investigating the "depth of mourning of what used to be" and discovering ways to celebrate a working-class past "without snickering."

Wolfgang Fritz Haug, in the second Remarx essay, takes issues with those "neo-Hegelian" readings of Marx according to which, after the *Grundrisse*, Marx attempted to popularize his theory and, as a result, moved away from the Hegelian dialectical method, thereby impoverishing his work. For Haug, in contrast, the changes Marx made—for example, in preparing the second edition of the first volume of *Capital*, in revising the French translation of the first volume, and composing the *Marginal Notes on Wagner*—attest to the fact that Marx's writings were a "work in progress." Perhaps even more important, they make the Marxian critique of political economy vital and open-ended and thus relevant to the "theoretical understanding of the emerging high-tech capitalism" of our time. Haug's careful scholarship (paying particular attention to what Marx *does* and less to what Marx *says* he does) describes the "improvements" Marx makes—in relating his concept of surplus labor to the everyday language of unpaid labor, in avoiding a relapse into speculative dialectics by referring to the determinate commodity, in explaining that his starting point was not the value-concept but the concrete commodity—as a reworking of his basic concepts "in the bright daylight of his workshop." Rather than the betrayal of a fixed method (that of Hegelian dialectics), what Haug sees in Marx's later texts is evidence of Marx's learning process: a "historical materialist rethinking of dialectics."

In the first of the three reviews that complete this issue, Chizu Sato enthusiastically endorses Suzanne Bergeron's critique of the key role a naturalized "national economy" has played in discussions of economic development, the state, and women in the post-World War II period. Sato focuses particular attention on three aspects of Bergeron's analysis: her challenging of the tendency of experts (from both mainstream and radical strands of development economics) to blame others for not knowing how to manage national economies instead of seeing their own unwillingness to relinquish the status of detached, rational observers; her ability to see the "contradictory and heterogeneous processes" that make it difficult to conceive of the nation as a monolithic economic entity; and her intervention into feminist debates on globalization that continue to presume that capitalism is monolithic and singularly powerful. Sato concludes her review by suggesting that Bergeron's powerful critique would be complemented and extended by considering such issues as the diversity of class processes, the role governmentality plays for women in the global South, and how the rethinking of expertise might lead to the emergence of new, collaborative relationships with the very subjects of development.

Richard Wolff, for his part, expresses an appreciation for Stanley's Aronowitz's latest book not only because it is "smoothly written and readily accessible" but also because it achieves "an important current political intervention." Wolff credits Aronowitz with exposing how, within U.S. capitalism from the "Reagan Revolution" on, higher profits have come at the expense of fewer and worse jobs and that the deteriorating employment situation is neither a sign of efficiency nor a temporary aberration. In other words, Aronowitz successfully documents the "sustained assault on the U.S. working class" over the course of the last thirty years. Still, Wolff believes that two other issues deserve additional attention: the fact that real wages have suffered a sustained decline for the first time since the beginning of the nineteenth century, with deleterious effects on the working class and U.S. society as a whole; and the idea that neoliberalism is merely one form of capitalism (as against, for example, more state-led forms of capitalist development), thus challenging the Left to direct its opposition to capitalism across all its phases.

In the third and final review, of Peter Hitchcock's *Imaginary States*, Maria Markantonatou notes that Hitchcock uses the tools of cultural studies, sociology, and literary criticism, and takes up a wide range of both theoretical debates and Caribbean literary texts, to conduct an intricate, instructive, and truly interdisciplinary analysis of "cultural transnationalism." According to Markantonatou, Hitchcock refuses mainstream views of both economic globalization and global multiculturalism and, instead, explores the ways in which literature can be seen as reacting both to the formation of national identities and to the new "postcolonial exploitative forms" associated with contemporary global capitalism. For Markantonatou, one of Hitchcock's most important arguments is that posing a global culture alone as "decisive blow to global modes of economic exploitation" is both idealist and misleading. It remains necessary, therefore, to carefully examine the ways political identity and aesthetic representation continue to be imagined and reimagined in terms of the formation of the Nation.

For readers who are not able to attend RM06 (and for those participants who wish to recapture the moment), the conference web site (www.rethinkingmarxism2006.org) will soon include an archive of texts and photos from the sessions, cultural showings and exhibits, and many other stimulating events that are going to be staged in Amherst. In future issues of RM, we will publish presentations from the plenary sessions as well as book symposia and selected papers from panels and workshops on the extraordinary array of topics that will be taken up by the hundreds of students, scholars, and activists participating in RM06.

The Editors

RETHINKING MARXISM   VOLUME 18   NUMBER 4   (OCTOBER 2006)

Setting in Motion

curated and edited by Susan Jahoda and Jesal Kapadia

Setting in Motion is the title for the following collaborative and individual projects in film, animation, video, and texts. In curating these works we draw from Jacques Rancière's work on the politics of aesthetics. Rancière describes a logic that has situated and, paradoxically, grounded art's potential for disagreement or dissensus. Thus, as art becomes increasingly about issues described as occupying politics, it becomes less polemical. What is called for is a reshaping of the space that artistic practice occupies, enabling political art to be politically effective.

Together, these projects share an affective view of a global socio-political landscape, referenced through metaphor and fiction, perception, psychoanalysis, and corporeality. They address a broad range of content, utilizing diverse strategies—repetitions, reactualizations, restagings, and reenactments—within the genres of experimental, underground, and activist media.

As both curators and participating artists, we have included works that individually and collectively seek an alternative economy of vision. This imaginary reconfigures political artistic practice as embodied visuality, in relation to both history and contemporary culture.

ISSN 0893-5696 print/1475-8059 online/06/040476-48
© 2006 Association for Economic and Social Analysis
DOI: 10.1080/08935690600901186

Ayreen Anastas

Pasolini Pa* Palestine
Video, 51 minutes, 2005

Pasolini Pa* Palestine is an attempt to repeat Pasolini's trip to Palestine in his film, *Seeking Locations in Palestine for "The Gospel According to Matthew"* (1963). It adapts his script into a route map superimposed on the current landscape, creating contradictions and breaks between the visual and the audible, the expected and the real. The video explores the question of repetition. For Heidegger *Wiederholung* 'repetition, retrieval' is one of the terms he uses for the appropriate attitude toward the past. "By the repetition of a basic problem we understand the disclosure of its original, so far hidden possibilities." The project ventures a conversation and a dialogue with Pasolini, especially his *Poem for the Third World*. *Discutere* 'to smash to pieces' is the Latin source of dialogue, discussion. The piece does not criticize Pasolini, but reveals unnoticed possibilities in his thought and works back to the 'experiences' that inspired it. *Pasolini Pa* Palestine* was created in conjunction with the residency at Almamal Foundation in Jerusalem.

Video stills from 'Pasolini Pa* Palestine' by Ayreen Anastas

Ayreen Anastas was born in Bethlehem, Palestine. She relocated to Germany in 1989 for a DAAD scholarship where she studied architecture at the Technical University in Berlin until 1996. She is currently living in Brooklyn. She has taught at the Pratt Institute in Brooklyn, in its School of Architecture, since 1999, and is one of the primary organizers of the 16Beavergroup (www.16beavergroup.org), a loose artist community that functions as a social and collaborative space on 16 Beaver Street.

Anastas's recent artistic projects and exhibitions include *Pasolini Pa* Palestine*, filmed while at Almamal residency in Jerusalem in 2004 (shown at Homeworks III, Beirut 2005, and at Hebbel Theater, Berlin 2006), *m* of Bethlehem* (shown at Argos Festival in Brussels 2005 and at CCA Glasgow *In the Poem about love you don't write the word love* 2005), and collaborations with artist Rene Gabri (*By many means necessary, Camp Campaign, Artistalk, RadioActive, United We Stand*). Her practice engages with issues of public and political space, language, the everyday, and the question of Palestine.

Stephen Andrews

The Quick and the Dead
Looping animation, 1 minute 14 seconds, 2004

The Quick and the Dead is an animation based on the parable of Cain and Abel. It reinscribes the story using imagery from the current Iraq war.

Video stills from the 'Quick and the Dead' by Stephen Andrews

Stephen Andrews was born in 1956 in Sarnia, Ontario, Canada. He has exhibited his work in Canada, the United States, Brazil, Scotland, France, and Japan. He is represented in the collections of the National Gallery of Canada, as well as many private collections. His work deals with memory, identity, technology, and their representations in various media.

Gregg Bordowitz

Three Poems for Rethinking Marxism
2006

Here and Now

Depressed by fatigue, apathy obtained
More was exhausted than our convictions
The defeat of dialectics occurred
The critique of authorial presence
I recall "institutional critique"
Critique was the operative idea
Opposition had clarity of stakes
Today we oppose the wars, most of us
And we deplore the current government
Yet a sense of unity eludes us
Leading to different problematics:
Analyze the nature of religion
Explore art's connection to belief

Art World After Party

Where men stand watching other men shoot pool
Women dance wildly around, ecstatic
The bar scene last night as a depiction
Rings within rings of ritual pleasure
The native observer worked at his drink
Bitter lemon mixed with grainy beer fizz
Where siblings negotiate jealousy
Friends are also affectionate rivals
Freud's Totem and Taboo in full effect
Some are pregnant, others alcoholic
Wealth has fallen to a fortunate few
Critical attention has graced few more
No one wants to credit the role of luck
When we need to be held everywhere we go
Constantly held by the caress of art
In a bar called the Emergency Room
A girl in flowered pants dances samba
The music was all dance hall, beats pounding
Each finds her own idiom on the floor
The gay boy amidst the women flourished
The conjunction of billiards and dance
Tactics and strategy. Dialectics
We need game as we conduct energy
In the gallery we find consumption
We hear testimony of enslavement
Recall that slaves require their masters' rule
Focus hard on the angles of physics
Spectacular molecular displays
Each of us particles, plus or minus
All charges can be reversed on contact
Adjust to the brightness of projectors
Video projection is the new norm
Light between the sacred and the profane
A universal distinction structures
Where mystery is not the founding cause
When awe is not enough to organize
We must inquire about beliefs to know
Elementary forms of religion
Art has never rejected religion

Rites and propitiations are its form
We believe that something higher drives us
We refuse to acknowledge our beliefs
Still we dance and play as if it matters
Emotions available as matter
Every artwork is a bloody relic
As every opening is a service
Recognize this now as holy wars rage
Recognize that the mind requires faith
Beliefs are sentiments. They're not ideas
Human animals produce their culture
We produce consciousness collectively
Our affects are matters of ritual
No one chooses their own dance idiom
Representation no longer exists
Where embodiment is the key concern
Instead of representing we perform
So we prefer actions to protests
Find humility in our offerings
Become aware of universals
Open. Open to being together
With all our antagonisms intact
Siblings, lovers, rivals, friends, particles
Empathy isn't chosen, it's structural
The object of hate is the same of love
When the other touches me. Yes or no
Where the object is the self we touch pride
Humility is akin to hatred
Good or bad, context determines passions
Good or bad, passions elicit morals
Sensations are the fundamental cause
Strange how thoughts develop intensities
Vague impressions and ideas co-mingle
Thinking and doing aren't identical
Lemon and beer introduced make summer
Dancing seems somehow connected to rain
There are no necessary relations
We're at an opening to celebrate
Desire writing to a chilling end failed

To Artists

Who does not wish to achieve grace through art
By grace we mean freedom and agency
To ensure in every motion pleasure
Remaining inwardly safe to play
To control the conditions of craft
The means of producing our own efforts
And spend our energies generously
Die worthy of our body's exhaustion
As laborers of all kinds still struggle

Gregg Bordowitz (born 14 August 1964, Brooklyn, New York) is a writer and film and video maker. His films, including *Fast Trip Long Drop* (1993), *A Cloud In Trousers* (1995), *The Suicide* (1996), and *Habit* (2001), have been widely shown in festivals, museums, and movie theaters, and broadcast internationally. His writings have been published in anthologies such as *AIDS: Cultural Analysis, Cultural Activism, Queer Looks, Uncontrollable Bodies, Resolutions*, and numerous publications and journals, including *The Village Voice, Frieze, Artforum, American Imago, Art Journal, Documents*, and October. In spring 2002, Bordowitz had his first solo museum show at the Museum of Contemporary Art in Chicago. His book *The AIDS Crisis Is Ridiculous and Other Writings 1986–2003*, was published by MIT Press in the fall of 2004. For this recent collection, Bordowitz received the 2006 Frank Jewitt Mather Award from the College Art Association. In addition, he has received a Rockefeller Intercultural Arts Fellowship and a John Simon Guggenheim Memorial Fellowship, among other grants and awards. Bordowitz is a member of the faculty of the Film/Video/New Media Department at the School of the Art Institute of Chicago, and he is on the faculty of the Whitney Museum Independent Study Program.

Moyra Davey

PLAY

*The following text was created for a group exhibition called **Reality/Play** organized by Moyra Davey at Orchard (New York City), from June 4–30, 2006. This version has been slightly modified for **Setting in Motion**.*

When I told some friends about the idea for this show at Orchard several of them recommended Johan Huizinga's *Homo Ludens*, an erudite work about the centrality of play in culture. The most inspiring and ludic part of the book (for me) is a short passage concluding the author's introduction in which he cautions the reader not to expect from him expertise on every aspect of his subject. A writer, he maintains, must sometimes be a "raider" in fields insufficiently explored or studied, the desire to write overtaking the exigencies of learning. Huizinga explains: "To fill in all the gaps in my knowledge beforehand was out of the question. I had to write it now, or not at all. And I wanted to write." This impatience, even urgency around writing that Huizinga alludes to, is a testament to the sustaining powers such creative work affords, and it is a form of sustenance inextricably linked to pleasure and forms of play.

Roland Barthes in *The Pleasure of the Text* says: "The writer is someone who plays with his mother's body," I've long puzzled over that cryptic line, from a longer, even more cryptic passage in which Barthes talks about pleasure in relation to writing (and reading). He says this pleasure comes not from language, but from the *mother tongue*, thereby denying the symbolic of language and privileging the imaginary of the mother's body. In that same short paragraph he mentions, parenthetically, a psychoanalyst, three writers and a painter, all leads I could pursue if I wanted to decode the mystery of that line: "The writer is someone who plays with his mother's body". But I suspect the line is not meant to be decoded, and for now I want to write (even if I also don't want to . . .)

Writing (especially its beginnings) is a heart-quickening thrill precisely because it engages that area of anticipation and dread, desire and fear, the teetering on the edge of a gulf that Virginia Woolf described in relation to the novel. (Non-fiction was straightforward for Woolf: she started an essay with the certainty that "sooner or later a net of words . . . would come down on the idea" and allow her to compose her text, but a novel was something altogether more fraught, its outcome by no means guaranteed.) The gulf is the threshold moment of knowing that something might be created, plucked from non-existence, or not. It is also the moment where pleasure and gratification abut work, and the thrill has to do with putting something at risk, as in a game of chance. There is no desire without law, as Lacan would say.

But getting back to Barthes, here's one more thing, from a an interview he gave in 1977, that begins to inflect and illuminate the cryptic, poetic line about the writer and the body of the mother: "When we attach a lot of importance to certain networks of friendship it is because we're always trying to reproduce the utopia of a childhood space, that of the child playing around its mother. Ultimately, in an affective relationship, whether or not it's amorous, we always simulate a certain maternal space, a space of security which is, why not say it, a gift space." This evocation of a maternal radius extending into adulthood, into the grownup life of Barthes the writer, also suggests its reverse, the forceful pull backwards, reminding me of Melanie Klein, who said that all art-making is a form of reparation with the mother, and emboldens me to take (almost) literally Barthes' idea about writing and the body of the mother. Barthes via Klein leads me to intuit a space of loss where one can in turn lose oneself to a love of making.

What does all this have to do with an exhibition at Orchard (or for that matter, this project in *Rethinking Marxism*, Setting in Motion)? To close, this time via Winnicott: what matters in the play of children is "the *preoccupation* ... the near-withdrawal state ... akin to the concentration of older children and adults" (when they are writing, or taking a photograph or editing a video, for instance, and possibly experiencing that sense of unbounded time known as 'oceanic'). These notes, mostly on writing, but equally relevant to all forms of art making, literalize ideas around demand and play. They exemplify a certain kind of intense engagement and absorption that artists and writers avail themselves of, participate in, and on occasion find therein: pleasure, bliss, wonder, agency and perhaps a place that harks back to, conjures, the "space around the mother."

Moyra Davey is an artist and a photographer. She is the editor of *Mother Reader: Essential Writings on Motherhood* (Seven Stories Press, 2001), an anthology on maternal ambivalence and the intersection of motherhood and creative life, and of *The Problem of Reading* (Documents Books 2003). She is a member of Orchard, a cooperative gallery on New York's Lower East Side, and a 2004-05 recipient of an *Anonymous Was a Woman* award.

Ashley Hunt

I WON'T DROWN ON THAT LEVEE AND YOU AIN'T GONNA' BREAK MY BACK (The
Corrections Documentary Project)
Video, 31 minutes, 2006
With Xochitl Bervera of Friends and Family of Louisiana's Incarcerated Children;
Corinne Curry of Human Rights Watch; Althea Francois of the Southern Center for
Human Rights; Tamika Middleton of Critical Resistance; Malik Rahim of Common
Ground Collective

I WON'T DROWN began with an invitation to travel to New Orleans as part of a
delegation to investigate what happened at the Orleans Parish Prison during and after
Hurricane Katrina. What came up was not only a botched and deadly evacuation of
the prison, but a broader climate of racial tension and brutality throughout the state
response to the disaster, as what had broken down were not only the city's
infrastructure and services, but also the historical partitions that structure and
ensure its racial and economic hierarchies, keeping people "in their place." This
video chronicles how these hierarchies were maintained nonetheless through the
rhetoric of law enforcement and imprisonment.

Video stills from 'I WON'T DROWN ON THAT LEVEE AND YOU AIN'T GONNA BREAK MY BACK' by Ashley Hunt

A Fortification of Race

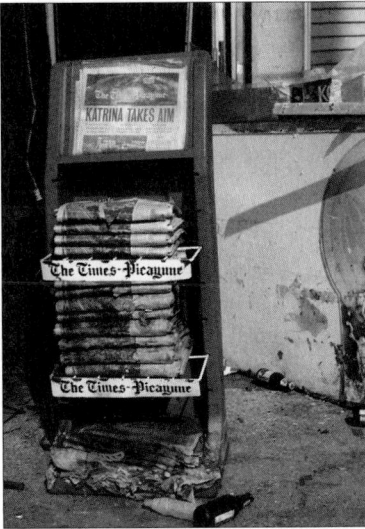

This morning I woke up in a curfew,
O God, I was a prisoner, too,
Could not recognize the faces standing over me,
They were all dressed in uniforms of brutality.

How many rivers do we have to cross,
Before we can talk to the boss?
All that we got, it seems we have lost
We must have really paid the cost.

(And that's why we'll be)
Burning and looting tonight,
Burning and looting tonight (to survive),
Burning all illusion tonight,
Burning all illusion tonight.

—Bob Marley, "Burnin' and Lootin'" (1973)

Newspaper rack and debris at corner store

Rumor had it that prisoners had been left to drown in their cells. More stories flowed out of New Orleans in the weeks after Hurricane Katrina, about the subsequent relocation of thousands of prisoners (many of whom had been simply awaiting trial) to prisons throughout Louisiana, where they were being held incommunicado. As an artist and activist who has worked in New Orleans a good deal, I was invited to join a delegation to the city, along with organizers, service providers, and human rights lawyers. This essay is part of a body of work that draws upon my days there, media coverage of the storm, and previous experiences within activism and politics in New Orleans.

Upon my arrival in New Orleans, I spoke with the woman I'd be staying with to ask if she might need anything. She said we'd need water in the house; could I find some? This was my first introduction to the necessity now governing the city, but also made me think years back to an interview I'd conducted with a former New Orleans Black Panther. When I'd asked why she was an activist, she recalled long months of having the water cut off in her house, images of scraping change together with her daughter and hauling empty jugs to the water dispenser at a local store.

As I recalled this driving into a deserted city, it would be only the first similarity to strike me between social destruction of poverty and racism, and the destruction brought by Hurricane Katrina. Considering the processes brought on by the storm, accelerated by the storm, and enacted by the state in response to the storm, I soon began to see their collected effects as analogous to ghettoization: the manifold processes that go into transforming a community into a ghetto.

Median strip on Broad Street at Canal Street

First, Hurricane Katrina wiped out what little infrastructure actually existed to support New Orleans communities before the storm, just as ghettoization destroys infrastructure, more slowly but surely, whether by economic divestment and strangulation or by bombs and bulldozers.

Second, Katrina revealed that an aspect of ghettoization is immobilization: the freezing of people and cordoning them off in their space. This was revealed in the immobilization of residents who could not afford to evacuate the city, who were literally stuck in the path of the storm, others who not allowed to cross over bridges out of the city into white suburbs, the curfews established, and the sealing off of the city after the storm had passed.

Third was the criminalization that was deployed by the state and media to characterize the city's remaining survivors as lawless and pathological (under the general label of "looting"). This characterization acts as a racialization, assigning a radical Other-ness to a group of people and naming them as an immanent threat that, by their very nature, need to be quarantined.

Fourth, extending from this racialized characterization, this dangerous otherness attached to the ghettoized residents, is the authorization for the state to act with violence upon them, so both their quarantine and the armed patrols in their streets and houses seem to be normal, or, at least, not outrageous.

Finally, this militarization reveals the spatial relationship between the state and a ghetto as one of militarized territorialization. Each of the preceding processes also belongs to this territorialization, manifest either as overt military occupation, which in New Orleans included bits and pieces of every imaginable military, policing, and imprisoning force in the United States (prison guards from around the United States were to be found in Louisiana), or indirect modes of occupation, such as antigang units, antidrug squads, extralegal policing squads, and public housing "safety" patrols.[1]

What this relation—enabled through racialization—might be compared to more generally is the *state of exception*, or *state of emergency*, the name given to any period of time when a state suspends its constitutional law: its obligations toward and respect for rights and protections (protections from state incursion), in response to a perceived danger. Giorgio Agamben has recently asserted that the state of exception is increasingly becoming the generalized condition of all states today.[2] In his writing about the "camp" (a close relative of the ghetto) as the definitive instance of such a space, he states:

> The camp is the space that is opened when the state of exception begins to become the rule ... [in the camp, the state of exception, which was essentially a temporary suspension of the rule of law on the basis of a factual state of danger, is now given a permanent spatial arrangement ...].[3]

That this "permanent spatial arrangement" is what "opens up" when the state of exception becomes the rule can be understood in at least two ways. First, the camp can be understood as a symbolic figure, wherein the camp is the total spatialization of a suspension of rights and a state without restriction. Second, in a more practical sense, it is one way we begin to see the state of exception manifest in our daily life, its first spatialization once implemented—not at all as an "exception" but as the beginning to the ruling principle to which we'll be submitted.

Collapsed house

This is why law firms of all political orientation have filed habeas corpus petitions for prisoners held incommunicado at Guantanomo Bay, including conservative firms: so as to prevent the state from opening up any such spaces in which people are rendered without rights and the state can act without limitation, what one such lawyer I've spoken with called a "legal black hole."

I would argue that this is precisely the rule and function of any ghetto, no matter what the justification for its implementation. More important, this was precisely the state's reaction to Hurricane Katrina in New Orleans: suspending rights and lawfulness (of the state) in order to establish the "security" of the state; it prioritized the integrity of the territory as *state territory* and protected the private property of select interests, both prior to saving and protecting people who are, at least in legal formality, citizens of that state.

The permanent institution of the state of exception already built into all modern governments is the prison, where the processes of the ghetto are concentrated and their effects contained. Through the logic of public safety and "deprivation of liberty," prisoners (primarily people raised their whole lives subjected to processes of ghettoization) are stripped of all but a minimum of human and civil rights, and are used to satisfy any number of needs of the state.

In New Orleans, the refusal to evacuate the Orleans Parish Prison was a claim to such exception, where prisoners were accorded the status of vermin: to be contained rather than rescued or acknowledged as human beings; their containment valued over their lives. Only after it had flooded horribly did the sheriff finally evacuate, while beginning the immediate construction of a chain-link fence jail behind the city's Greyhound Bus station. Looking a great deal like the Guantanomo Bay prison, it continued support for the state of exception and the larger ghettoization of the city: a holding space for storm victims not regarded as victims, but rounded up by police and military for looting, curfew violations, and charges that can be understood as "poor laws."[4] In this way, rather than fulfilling their avowed civil function, prisons tend to function as ghettos of a ghetto, where the negligence and violence of ghettoization, and the responding social disorder and dissidence, are disappeared and the generalized criminalization of the ghettoized is accomplished.

As this condition was not only the response to a storm but was also the history of New Orleans, it brings to light what we see in communities throughout this country and the world, where more and more, communities and cultures are demonized and cinched off economically; surrendered of their rights and protections; categorized as immanent threats by virtue of the criminality or dangerousness projected onto them as their inherent "nature." Everywhere, under varied rationales, we see communities living under permanent states of exception: policed rather than served by the police; subjects of control, inspection, and detention rather than subjects of politics; for whom the state is a militarizing and surveilling force authorized by the discourses of the War on Crime, the War on Drugs, and increasingly, the War on Terror—all of which can be understood as post–Civil Rights era discourses of race-making, each of which is inherently raciological and racializing.

At this point, however, I should back up and say that none of this is really so simple, and it points to a certain inadequacy of the neat and tidy categories of race and class as they've been simplified in our popular and political discourses. Whatever authorized the social and political destruction of Katrina must have been much deeper and more complex than mere prejudice or derisive sentiment, as racism is generally located today, especially when we are asked to untangle race from class.

It is essential to point out that what fell away during Katrina was not just New Orleans's civil structure and infrastructure, but also the built and socialized spatializations of race and class hierarchy that are New Orleans's history (as they are of every place). Beneath superficial attitudes of racism is the ordering of space and experience—in the partitions of space, social habits and physical architectures—which are the major technology of how race and class continue to be regulated, hierarchized, and policed; the every day fortifications which control the racial Other and "keeps them in their place," of which the ghetto is just one expression.

Importantly, such spatializations are not only what *regulates* race, but are *how race exists*. As the theorists of spatial practices teach us that there is no social or political relation that does not have a spatial corollary or manifestation, it can also be said that such corollaries are not *additions to* a relation, but are in fact the very *location* of that relation—how and where that relation can and does take place. Since race is not a biological fact, but is a social fiction which is always in crisis, the building and territorializing of space is not only how race is "enacted" but is in fact how race *can be;* space preserves not only the proper ordering of race, but inasmuch as these structures are also symbolic, it maintains the illusion of race as a stable reality altogether.

Once Katrina wiped out the material mechanisms and practices that had kept the black and poor communities of New Orleans "in their place" for centuries, it took with it these symbolic markers of racial stability and control, leaving only the racial imagination, which, for its own stability and affirmation, needs to perceive the neat separation of one group from another; to perceive a *self* that is "safe" from that *other*, or deeper, simply *distinct* from its Other. What happens when the stability of the distinction between one racially based identity loses the terrain upon which it knows itself, sees itself as protected from its Other, and ultimately loses the markers that separate itself identifiably from its Other?

New Orleans District Attorney's Office with car

One place to look is to much of the hysteria that took place during Katrina, specifically the irrational fear throughout the outlying suburbs that hordes of "animalistic black people" were coming to rush over the bridges from New Orleans to loot and ravage entire white communities.[5] Or we can consider the untruths that the sheriff's and police departments themselves announced about marauding gangs of black youth in the streets, murders and rapes in the Superdome and Convention Center, none of which have since been substantiated as anything other than rumors, yet never explained.[6]

What was to account for these rumors spread by law enforcement themselves, beyond the possibility they had spread them to justify the use of paramilitary force or to garner extra resources? Both these explanations are likely but, alone, fall short, for they do not account for how predisposed the general public was to embrace such rumors, or how easily the rumors came to characterize the whole of the situation in New Orleans to the public that was audience to the disaster throughout the United States.

> [W]hen the colonist speaks of the colonized he uses zoological terms. Allusion is made to the slithery movements of the yellow race, the odors from the "native" quarters, to the hordes, the stink, the swarming, the seething, and the gesticulations . . . This explosive population growth, those hysterical masses, those blank faces, those shapeless, obese bodies . . . all this is part of the colonial vocabulary. (Franz Fanon, *The Wretched of the Earth*)

Perhaps these examples were not only a mixture of strategic desire and paranoid fear of an unleashed, mythological "black horde," which Fanon helps us to situate as a figure of the Western racial imagination. Perhaps, upon the disintegration of the symbolic structures that would "hold back" this racial figure, these were reifications of the catalogue of that imagination, unleashed in the very real form of hysterical hallucinations. In such a traumatic environment, the likelihood of such hysteria was real, and asks us to push past simple calculations of race and class prejudice, toward the breakdown of figures of knowledge that belong to a broader ordering of social life.

Katrina and its aftermath revealed not just an intersection of race and class as two separate things unto themselves, but rather, overlapping discourses that claim common as well as opposing objects, both producing a truth effect that categorizes groups of people as generally mad—a labeling that renders those labeled as less than fully human and illegible as subjects. Michel Foucault begins his *Madness and Civilization*:

> We have yet to write the history of that other form of madness, by which men, in an act of sovereign reason, confine their neighbors, and communicate and recognize each other through the merciless language of non-madness.

In the case of New Orleans, I'm not referring to the storm as having "driven people crazy," although it certainly did. I mean madness as a limit line, a threshold which was exposed, on one side of which lies the figure of civilization, and on the other is the projection of madness that Foucault describes as the "constitutive outside" of that civilization, against which "civilization" can know itself.

Foucault describes a socially produced split between reason and nonreason, where nonreason constitutes this othered outside, whereupon it is converted into an object of scientific inquiry, an inquiry that is barred from ever referring back to that original split or its social or political character, leaving its division already natural, unquestionable, a priori. He writes:

> What is constitutive is the action that divides madness, and not the science elaborated once this division is made and calm restored. What is originative is the caesura that establishes the distance between reason and non-reason; reason's subjugation of non-reason, wresting from it its truth as madness, crime, or disease, derives explicitly from this point.

In New Orleans, where we saw "survivor" written onto the bodies of some people (primarily white), we saw the figure of "looter" mapped onto others. This was by no means assigned only to people who'd transgressed private property law but was drawn in broad strokes onto swaths of bodies that appeared already to the racialized gaze of "civilization" as markers of the irrational, the uncontrollable, of chaos. While the former were recognized as civilization's own members, legible as citizens to be saved, the latter was split off, written out of this possibility by the projection of madness onto them—the madness which, in our society, is written through discourses of race, class, gender, and sexuality, producing them as Other, imbuing them with threat, chaos, disorder, the pathological, dishonest and simple.

This "originative" split is a discursive operation that distributes bodies respectively to one side or other: while on one side are the sane—people legible and audible as legitimate political subjects—on the other are the mad—people illegible, rendered silent, politically muted. Incapable of speech, they become instead subjects to a culture's discourses of truth, of its "science[s] elaborated once this division is made," which cannot hear them but can only study them in monologue. Foucault continues:

> [O]n one hand, the man of reason delegates the physician to madness, thereby authorizing a relation only through the abstract universality of disease ... [this] posits the separation as already effected, and thrusts into oblivion all those stammered, imperfect words without fixed syntax in which the exchange between madness and reason was made. The language of psychiatry, which is a monologue of reason *about* madness, has been established only on the basis of such a silence.

Media and political analysis were precisely such monologues during Katrina, the primary "sciences" taking the "mad" as their object, articulating their "disease" as crime. This mirrored the larger state of our society in which no longer a physician, but the police chief, warden, and district attorney are "delegated to madness," thereby, shifting Foucault's terms, "authorizing a relation to the mad through the abstract universality" of *criminality and dangerousness;* projecting madness, but along with it, all that is wrong with or challenging in society. Put in the colonial context, Fanon continues:

"Military helicopter"

> The colonial world is a Manichaean world ... the colonist turns the colonized
> into a kind of quintessence of evil ... The "native" is declared impervious to
> ethics, representing not only the absence of values but also the negation of
> values. He is, dare we say it, the enemy of values.

What looking to Katrina can push us to consider is a more careful read of this split
between madness and reason, a concocted dividing line whose original split is barred
from recognition, as it resembles, or is perhaps structurally archetypal to, the split
that marks so many forms of subjugation which are explained through vocabularies of
madness and irrationality. We can think of how this permeates the history of
discourses of race, from supremacist texts that argue genetic bases for intellectual
and moral inferiority of people of color, to more recent texts that have argued
the same on sociological bases, to current discussions that blame stubborn,
"nonassimilated" black culture and familial structure for their own poverty, such as
those of John McWhorter of the Manhattan Institute.[7]

We could also trace the use of madness in the historical subjugation of women and
policing of gender, wherein modes of resistance, intellectuality, self-defense, and
rejection of gender codes are attributed to hysteria, or the "devil in the womb."
Phyllis Chesler, for example, in her book *Women and Madness*, documents a variety of
manifestations of this, including historical accounts of women confined to mental
asylums by their husbands for having been disagreeable or unruly, resisting sex, being
in the way of an affair, or any number of other ways of inconveniencing husbands
and fathers.[8]

Another obvious place to look is discourses on queerness and non-normative sexual
identity that construe same-sex desire as pathological. It was only in 1986 that the
American Psychiatric Association removed homosexuality from its *Diagnostic and*

Statistical Manual of Mental Disorders (DSM), whereas the World Health Organization only ended its classification of homosexuality as a mental disorder in 1992.

Add to these the production of the Other common to any historical case of genocide, and the dehumanizing rationales that have been operative in slave societies, and we have at least a partial list of such instances, one that begins to situate Katrina within long and varied histories of subjugation which are perhaps not so distinct in their mechanics. The state's response to Katrina expressed madness through the discursive figures of race and class—interwoven in a projection of madness, but also as an *expression* of madness (as Foucault wrote of the "madness" in "acts of sovereign reason") and ultimately, a *cause* of so much madness. Despite the sympathy that Katrina's images inspired, whether they could ultimately be read as human suffering is an important question, since they were understood first as racialized chaos and disorder. More than any overwhelming threat to private property or "the rule of law," this perception of madness in the form of a racial crisis is why the state's response was definitively one of violence, territorialization, containment, and quarantine, excusing a generalized state of exception that is instrumental to the goals and processes of ghettoization.

This brings us to the final stage of ghettoization, which is no longer ghettoization. What follows is the final removal of the ghettoized, argued through racialization, authorized by the state of exception, and setting the stage for *gentrification*. Accordingly, right-wing think tanks, pundits, and blogs praised the "unintended consequences" of the storm as a much needed cleansing of the city's "criminal elements." It takes no stretch of the imagination to consider what the benefit would be to the powerful interests of the city and region if these populations—perceived in their inhumanity as a scourge and obstacle to profits—were erased. Clearing the way for expanded tourism, breaking up one of the only black voting blocs in the state, and the redevelopment of eminent domain property lots, seized from those who cannot make it back to the city, are but three obvious motivations to consider.[9] And now the first post-Katrina census of New Orleans has been publicized, whereupon Ray Nagen's P-Funk predictions are sounding increasingly hollow.[10] The census reveals the city's black majority has dwindled from two-thirds to just fifty-five percent, while its

Public housing unit and boat at the Calliope Projects

median income rose by ten percent. Embedded more clearly in the interesting statistic that the number of households *without access to vehicles* has declined by more than half,[11] is a clear sign that Katrina has already made New Orleans richer and whiter, a disturbingly successful gain for those who envision a total cleansing of poor and black people from the city, wherein conditions of ghettoization lay the groundwork for gentrification, and meet ultimately with historical modes of banishment and exile from city gates.

It is a grim picture, but it is so far a grim history. If I were to offer hope, it would not be to first seek reform of the government or "enlighten" the racial vision of society. Instead, I see hope within the autonomous grass-roots organizing that has taken place in the city, stopping home demolitions, documenting police and jail abuses, creating independent media, and rehabbing houses so as to help bring back people who can't afford to rebuild.[12] Ultimately they are working on the principle that power is not uniform, unidirectional, or univocal, nor is it ever "completed" forever in its monopoly, which those who live with necessity, by necessity, already know. Hope is in the power that belongs to those categorized as mad, rendered illegible, muted, or in Ralph Ellison's terms, invisible (not in what is offered to them); it is in the ability of social movements to convert the energies and strategies already in the service of daily survival—and those used to subjugate them—into their own political power.
"I myself, after existing some twenty years, did not become alive until I discovered my invisibility," claims the nameless narrator of Ellison's *Invisible Man*. Despite the torment of his invisibility, he finds power and autonomy within it as well, while teaching us of the madness to be found in the position that claims a monopoly of reason. Recall the haunting passage of the story's prologue, in which arrogant insults flung at him by a white man summon the violent rage of a lifetime of racial attacks, so that he nearly slits the man's throat. "Oh yes I kicked him! And in my outrage I got out my knife and prepared to slit his throat." But in an epiphany of both his own power over this oppressor and the nature of that vision that renders him invisible, he stops himself, realizing that the man was, "as far as he knew . . . in the midst of a walking nightmare!" He continues:

> Then I was amused: Something in this man's thick head had sprung out and beaten him within an inch of his life. I began to laugh at this crazy discovery.

As James Baldwin describes whiteness as ultimately a dependent to its exoticized and demonized Other, or as Orlando Patterson declares the master a parasite living off the slave, rather than the reverse, the arrogance that valorizes domination is always a misrecognition of both itself and the dominated. It is always a distorted vision, blind to the power it invests in its Other, whereas the power and energy exercised by a dominant group becomes, in itself, a potential source of power to be amassed and organized by those subjected. Before political demands of legibility and recognition, voice and inclusion, there must be self-organization and self-definition, buoyed by the reminder that no dominated subject is precisely what an oppressor fantasizes that temporarily dominated subject to be. In the words of Ellison's narrator:

> It is incorrect to assume that, because I'm invisible and live in a hole, I am dead . . . Call me Jack-the-Bear, for I am in a state of hibernation . . . Please, a

definition: hibernation is a covert preparation for a more overt action ... I believe in nothing if not action.

1. In New Orleans's public housing developments these mysterious police squads are called the "Safe Home" force, which to the (now former) residents of these developments was nothing short of cynical and a source of laughter.

2. I regard Walter Benjamin's assertion that "the state of emergency is the exception but the rule" important here as an expression of the latent desire of all states to be unrestrained, unaccountable, and totalitarian, and when not forced to do otherwise, will act accordingly. Hence, when Agamben states, "when the state of exception begins *to become* the rule," I distinguish this from Benjamin's assertion in that it is referring to the actual, practical implementation of constitutional law's suspension—fulfilling that latent impulse.

3. Georgio Agamben, *Homo Sacer*, 1998; also see Agamben, *State of Exception*, 2005.

4. For discussion of the history of class and criminal codes, see *The London Hanged: Crime and Civil Society in the Eighteenth Century*, by Peter Linebaugh, 2001; also see the ACLU of New Orleans's report on coerced plea bargains forced upon many arrested, exchanging guilty pleas for reduced sentences of community service, cleaning out the flooded jail and courthouse.

5. Although there's no way to categorize the intentions behind the fivefold increase in background checks for gun purchases the FBI documented in the month after Katrina, the only places people near New Orleans could buy guns were in the outlying, white suburbs. Similarly, the Chief of Police for Westwego County told National Public Radio that he'd authorized $18,000 in new weapons purchases to protect against looters in a town where there was no looting.

6. Despite the perception of the hurricane, for months after Katrina the last homicide officially recorded by the police had been on 27 August, two days before the hurricane hit. See Adam Nossiter, *International Herald Tribune*, 11 November 2005.

7. For an excellent recounting of this intellectual history, see Clyde Woods, *Development Arrested: Race, Power, and the Blues in the Mississippi Delta*, Verso, 1998, or his forthcoming revision, Development Arrested: From the Plantation Era to the Katrina Crisis in the Mississippi Delta, 2007.

8. Phyllis Chesler, *Women and Madness*, 1972, 2002.

9. For a more thorough elaboration, see Mike Davis, "Gentrifying Disaster," http://www. zmag.org/content/showarticle.cfm?SectionID = 72&ItemID = 8992; and Naomi Klien, "The Rise of Disaster Capitalism," *The Nation*, 2 May 2005.

10. Gulf Coast Impact Estimates, U.S. Census Bureau, http://www.census.gov/acs/www/Products/Profiles/ gulf_coast/tables/tab1_katrinaK0100US2203v.htm; http://www.census.gov/Press-Release/www/ emergencies/gulfcoast_impact_estimates.xls.

11. http://www.census.gov/acs/www/Products/Profiles/gulf_coast/tables/tab4_ katrinaK0100US2203v.htm.

12. Visit the Web sites for the Common Ground Collective (http://www.commongroundrelief. org), the People's Hurricane Relief Fund (http://www.peopleshurricane.org), Hurricane Autonomous Workers Collective (http://www.peoplesfreespace.org/hurricanerelief), and New Orleans Independent Media Center (http://neworleans.indymedia.org).

Ashley Hunt is an artist, activist, and writer who works with video, mapping, and installation to engage the ideas of social movements, modes of learning, and public discourse. His primary work of the past eight years has been the development of *The Corrections Documentary Project* (www.correctionsproject. com), which deals with the contemporary growth of prisons as central to today's wealth accumulation and racial exclusion. Hunt's work has been exhibited at the Martin Luther King Jr. Center in Atlanta, the Contemporary Museum in Baltimore, Kunst-Werke Institute for Contemporary Art in Berlin, as well as numerous grass-roots and community-based venues throughout the United States. Other writings can be found in the *Journal of Aesthetics and Protest* (2005), *Sandbox Magazine* (2002) and at Artwurl.org (2003–present). He is currently a fellow at the Vera List Center for Art and Politics, and lives in Los Angeles where he teaches at the University of California at Irvine.

Susan Jahoda

... of a worm in a pomegranate
Video, 15 minutes, 2006

Subjects organize their sense of *being* through time and space. Time and space are a complex weave of public impositions, socially instituted affects and representations, and an imaginary, shaped by its own unconscious rhythms. *... of a worm in a pomegranate* explores the ways in which subjects internalize, cohabitate with, and creatively experience institutional time and space in an attempt to negotiate agency. In one continuous video capture, light at dusk passes from one interior wall to another. This image provides the visual component of a nonsequential narrative that calls upon topics ranging from phantom limb phenomena to global warming.

Video stills from '... of a worm in a pomegranate' by Susan Jahoda

Susan Jahoda is an interdisciplinary artist, art co-editor for *Rethinking Marxism*, and professor at the University of Massachusetts, Amherst. Her work includes photography, performance, installation, and video. She has been the recipient of grants and awards, including fellowships from the National Endowment and the New York Foundation for the Arts, and her work has been exhibited and published widely in Europe and North America. Current projects in video and sound explore how subjects can make claims for psychic and social belonging, in a location between time and space as constituted in and by the body, and time and space as situated in the world.

Jesal Kapadia

This is not a ...
Video, 2 minutes 30 seconds, 2003

Probing the legacy of surrealism, particularly to Rene Magritte's famous painting *'Ceci n'est pas une pipe,' This is not a ...* attempts to unravel the European avant-garde in the context of global diasporic circulations. The short video performs an ambivalent homage to three ordinary objects used commonly in an Indian household: a coconut grater, a tongue cleaner, and the idli-mold. These everyday instruments also border on the uncanny, displaced from their familiar context of use into a sparse white environment.

The soundtrack consists of three musical pieces, which are devotional love songs that have no connection with the everyday character of the 'not objects'. Do they invest the stainless steel objects with a sense of nostalgia, reverence, and even fetishistic desire, or is it that the text is ironic toward this disproportionate affective investment in the objects?

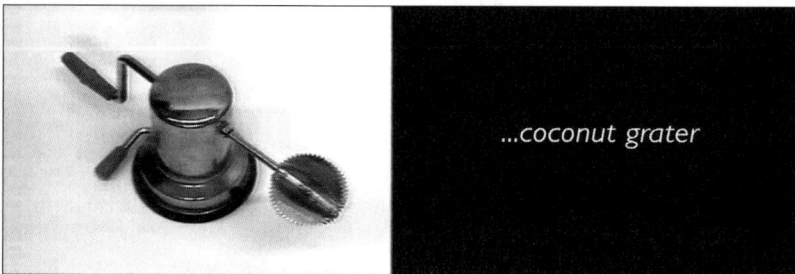

...coconut grater

Video stills from 'This is not a ...' by Jesal Kapadia

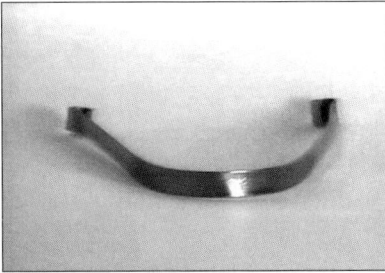

...tongue cleaner

...idli mould.

Jesal Kapadia is an artist from Mumbai, India, now living in New York City. Her work has primarily been in the genre of experimental video and digital print media. Using a tactical approach in developing her projects, the experience of migration with its effects on the human body, psyche, and imagination is what she questions and represents in her work. Drawing from moments in the history of the avant-garde, particularly surrealism, and incorporating ideas from postcolonial feminist theory, her work explores alternative modernities emerging in India and its diaspora.

Jesal Kapadia is also the art co-editor for *Rethinking Marxism* and a recipient of a Massachusetts Cultural Council grant for film and video artists. Her work has been shown at various venues: Experimenta '05 & '06 Film Festival in Mumbai, SENI International Visual Arts Festival in Singapore, Contemporary Arts Center in Lithuania, MIT's Media Test Wall at the List Visual Arts Center, Momenta Art in Brooklyn, New York, Socrates Sculpture Park in Long Island City New York, Vera List Center for Arts and Politics at the New School University, Art in General in New York and most recently at Artists Space, New York. She currently teaches at the International Center of Photography and CUNY College of Staten Island in New York City and Rhode Island School of Design in Providence.

Lin + Lam

Departure
Video, 48 minutes, 2006

Departure is a video essay that looks at the impact of modernization and foreign intervention through different modes of transportation. Shot from the exploratory perspective of a moving car, cycle, and trains, the video travels through three former colonial Asian cities: Taipei, Shanghai, and Hanoi. The transformation of a road, a bridge, and railways, shows an evolution of different powers marked by the promise of progress made by former occupiers and current builders.

In recognition of language hierarchies and the politics of translation, five women narrate the interrelated histories of these transforming urban environments in their native languages: Mandarin Chinese, Taiwanese, English, Shanghainese, and Vietnamese.

Video stills from 'Departure' by Lin + Lam

Through critical narratives, Lin + Lam's collaborative work examines how individual and national subjectivities are mediated and defined. For the past four years, they have produced work that has extended from researching questions of democracy and representation. They have participated in group shows at ARTSPEAK, Vancouver, British Columbia, the Vera List Center for Art and Politics, the New School, New York, rum46 exhibition space, Århus, Denmark, and The Economist Gallery, Hong Kong. Their first collaborative video, *Departure*, premiered at the Asian Vision Competition of the Taiwan International Documentary Festival. In fall 2006, they will have a solo show at Gallery 456, New York, where they will present a mixed media installation that deals with propaganda and the relationship between the United States and South Vietnam.

Paying close attention to materiality, site, and the specificities of different media, Lin + Lam integrate their individual strengths and backgrounds. H. Lan Thao Lam uses photography, sculpture, and installation to probe the construction of history and lived places. She has received a Canada Council for the Arts Grant, H. L. Rous Sculpture Award, Owen W. Wilson Memorial Award, James Robertson Environmental Design Award, and Sully Corth Memorial Fund. She has taught at Middle Tennessee State University and Goddard College in Plainfield, Vermont. Lana Lin's films, videos, and installations have interpreted different cultural contexts, raising questions about translation and the processes of identification. Her work has been shown at the Museum of Modern Art and the Whitney Museum of American Art, in New York, as well as at the Festival de Femmes, Creteil, France, and the London Film Festival, England. She has been awarded numerous fellowships, including the New York State Council on the Arts, The Jerome Foundation, the U.S. Fulbright Foundation, and the Civitella Ranieri Foundation in Umbria, Italy.

Ulrike Müller

LOVE/TORTURE
Video, 6 minutes, 2005

LOVE/TORTURE performs a text about pain and pleasure—sexualized but not necessarily shared pleasure. It investigates emotional relationships and the contemporary subjectivities of media consumers. Confronted with both the bleakly simple (people are torturing and killing, people are being tortured and killed) and the utterly confusing (people are torturing and killing, people are being tortured and killed), this video proposes that viewers shift their attention to identify with the role of the perpetrator rather than with the victim.

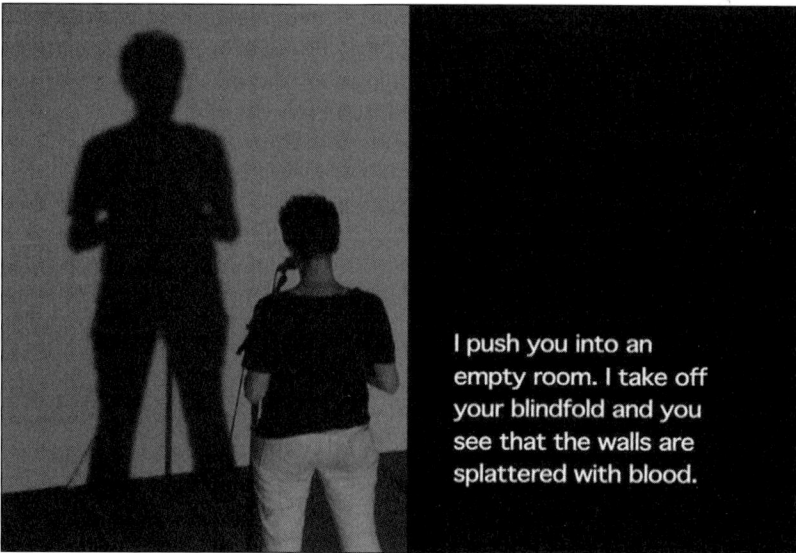

I push you into an empty room. I take off your blindfold and you see that the walls are splattered with blood.

Video stills from 'LOVE/TORTURE' by Ulrike Müller

You wake up as your head hits the floor. Your skull bounces off the concrete and you are surprised by its elasticity. For a moment, you don't know who you are and what I am doing to you. I punch you in the chest so hard that you almost go into cardiac arrest.

I see the terror in your eyes. You are mine and deep down you know. You slowly back up towards the door. You don't know I locked it. There is no way out for you, and besides you would not be happy out there. I am all you need and you belong to me.

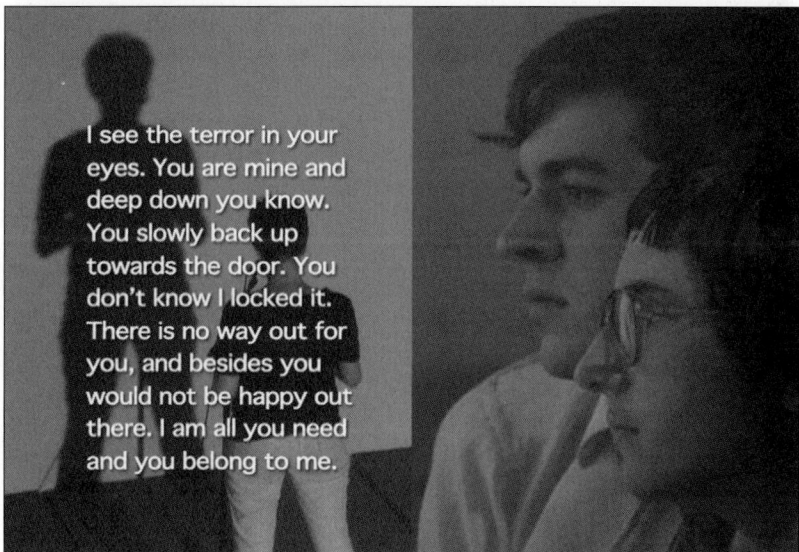

Ulrike Müller is an artist currently living and working in New York. Since 2005 she has been an editor for the queer feminist art journal *LTTR* (www.lttr.org). Exhibitions, performances, and video screenings include Ridykeulous (New York, 2006), Diagonale, Festival of Austrian Film (Graz, 2005), and Mothers of Invention—Where Is Performance Coming From (Mumok, Vienna, 2003). The artist's book *Every little bit helps—Ulrike Müller: Two Audio Works* (2005, with essays by Bordowitz, Barbara Schröder, Lanka Tattersall, and Walter Johnston) is distributed by Revolver (www.revolver-books.de) Printed Matter (printedmatter.org).

Jenny Perlin

Possible Models
16mm, b/w, silent, 10 minutes 45 seconds, 2004

The 16mm b/w hand-drawn film, *Possible Models,* begins by outlining a news story about John Ashcroft's announcement in June 2004 that a Somali immigrant to Columbus, Ohio (my home state), was charged with plotting to blow up a mall. The Somali, Nuradin Abdi, was arrested in November 2003, and held for more than six months before being formally charged. Ashcroft's announcement of this case came on 14 June 2004, a day before U.S. presidential candidate, Senator John Kerry, was scheduled to speak in Columbus. The film continues with three parts.

Part 1 describes the idealistic vision of Victor Gruen, designer of the first shopping mall in the United States, and his failed project of creating a better world through the construction of communities in the newly forming suburbs of the United States. Part 2 compares two megamalls: the Mall of America in Minnesota, which is the largest mall in the United States, with the hyper-megamall currently under construction in Dubai, United Arab Emirates. This mall complex, called the Mall of Arabia, is part of Dubailand, a Disneyland-type complex that magnifies the possibilities of consumption and controlled experience beyond anything yet constructed. Part 3 addresses the current development of the "Freedom Ship," a floating community of the wealthy that will slowly and continuously circumnavigate the globe. The Freedom Ship will take about three years to go around the world, and is a completely self-contained community, including schools, parks, casinos, malls, and an airplane landing strip and marina for residents' ships and planes. The Freedom Ship will dock off various countries around the world, so residents can go out and consume 'local' experiences and visitors can come and admire the floating city. The Freedom Ship is also a zone where the privilege of the wealthy means that their lives will no longer be subject to taxation. Finally, the film concludes with the continuation of the story of the Somali immigrant, the consequences of his escape from the brutal wars in his country, the new life he built in Ohio, and the possibility of what awaits him in the courts of the United States.

Video still from 'Possible Models' by Jenny Perlin

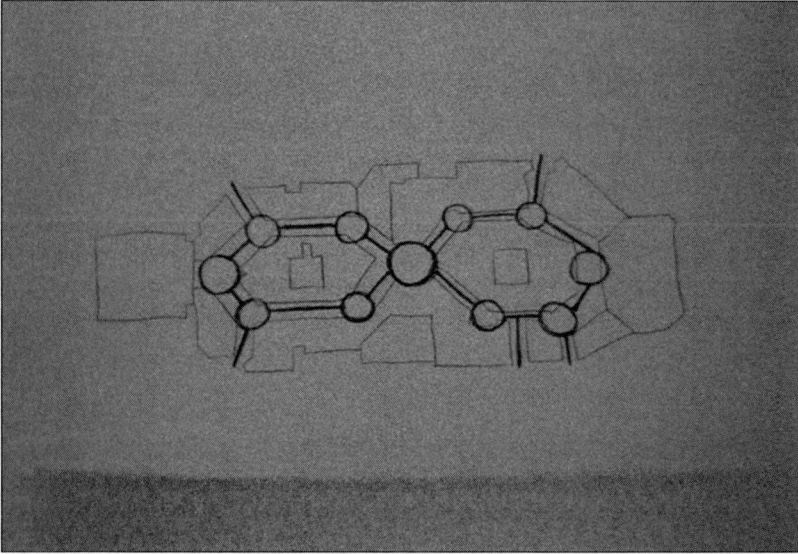

Jenny Perlin's 16mm films, videos, and drawings work with and against the documentary tradition, incorporating innovative stylistic techniques to emphasize issues of truth, misunderstanding, and personal history. Perlin's films and installations have been shown at the Rotterdam Film Festival, the Whitney Museum of American Art, the Berlin International Film Festival, the Ann Arbor, Black Maria, and Images festivals, Pacific Film Archive, P.S. 1/MoMA, KunstWerke, Berlin, the Drawing Center, Centre d'art Contemporaine, Geneva, the Renaissance Society, Chicago, the Aldrich Museum, the Queens Museum, Galerie M+R Fricke, Düsseldorf, Kunsthalle Exnergasse, Vienna, and Annet Gelink Gallery, Amsterdam. Grants and fellowships have included an Arnold Foundation grant for independent film production in the Czech and Slovak Republics, two CEC/Artslink Grants for collaborative film and art projects in Eastern Europe (with Sarah Jane Lapp and Trebor Scholz), an Experimental Television Center Grant, and a New York State Council on the Arts grant. She is represented by Annet Gelink Gallery, Amsterdam. Jenny Perlin was born in Williamstown, Massachusetts. She studied film and cultural studies at Brown University (B.A., 1993), completed her M.F.A. in film at the School of the Art Institute of Chicago (1998), and did postgraduate studies at the Whitney Independent Study Program in New York (1999).

Emily Roysdon

POW
Video, 1 minute 30 second loop, 2006

"Do what?" speaks the collapsed subject. Rise again, midway through a tangible loop. Respond again to the textual transformation. Untitled/POW is a body forward meditation on repetitive movements and recurring powers. It draws a relationship between the 'act of writing' and the 'out-of-frame' forces that are given voice, as well as the ambiguous violence this tension enacts on the affected subject. Beginning in a cloud of palimpsest, the video enters a performative space that bears the remainder of inscription and erasure. Is the text effecting the collapse? Substituting for a body of control? Or, in fact, is it a revelation?

Video still from 'POW' by Emily Roysdon

Emily Roysdon is a Los Angeles- and New York-based interdisciplinary artist whose projects engage language and memory. Imaging collectivity and communicability as metonymic structures, her projects try to simultaneously exhibit ecstatic resistance and structural collapse. She is also an editor and cofounder of LTTR, a feminist genderqueer artist collective with a flexible project-oriented practice. LTTR produces an annual independent art journal, performance series, events, screenings, and collaborations. Roysdon's work has been shown at *Freedom Salon*, Deitch Projects, New York; MIT List Visual Art Center, Cambridge; Longwood Arts Project, Bronx; The Kitchen, New York; Art in General, New York; and Contemporary Art Centre, Vilnius, Lithuania. Roysdon completed the Whitney Museum Independent Study Program in 2001 and an interdisciplinary M.F.A. at the University of California Los Angeles in 2006.

Jason Simon

Vera
Video, 25 minutes, 2006

Vera is an assisted self-portrait of consumption. The subject is a woman whose passions and compulsions are of spending and loss, taste and subjectivity. The video consists entirely of an interview in which Simon's questions are first audible, then excised, and Vera herself never leaves the screen. Along with *Production Notes: Fast Food for Thought* (1987) and *Paul Schrader's Bag* (1994–2004), Simon's work investigates relationships between consumption and our shared formations of the self.

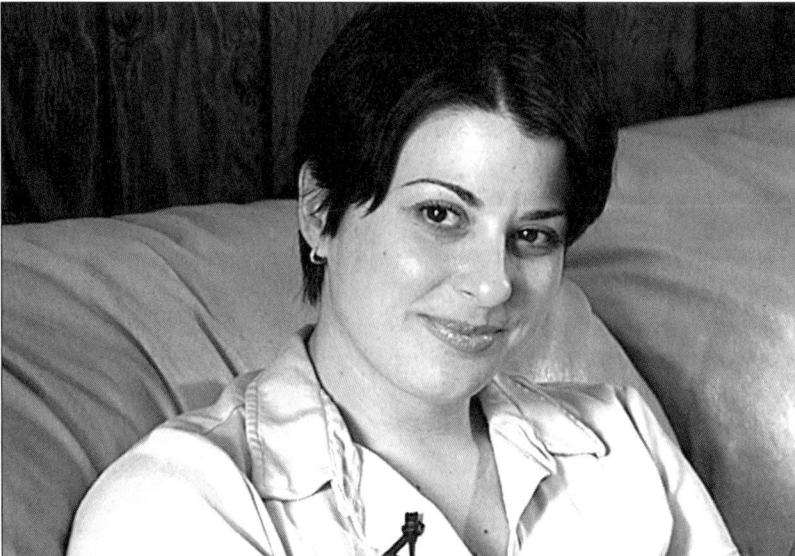

Video still from 'Vera' by Jason Simon

Jason Simon is an artist and film and video maker based in New York City. He is a founding member of the cooperative gallery Orchard and an associate professor of cinema at the College of Staten Island, City University of New York. He has shown his work in the Whitney Biennial and in solo gallery shows at Pat Hearn Gallery and American Fine Arts Co., and his writing has appeared in journals such as *Parkett, Purple, Springerin,* and *Frieze.* His films and videos are distributed by The Video Data Bank, First Run/Icarus Films, and some of his projects deal with advertising, art restoration, public address systems, and collecting. He is the recipient of grants from Art Matters Inc., The Polaroid Foundation, The Washington State Arts Council, and The New York Foundation for the Arts. He worked with Bill Horrigan at the Wexner Center for the Arts establishing the Wexner's Art & Technology lab, and has curated film and video programs in New York and abroad. Each summer he hosts the one-day, one-minute film and video festival in a barn in upstate New York with his partner Moyra Davey. *Vera* premiered at Orchard and in the exhibition "Capital (it fails now)" in 2006.

Speculative Archive (Julia Meltzer and David Thorne)

Talking oneself out of a corner out of the corner of one's mouth
Multichannel video projection, work in progress, 2006
Excerpts from *Syria Kubra,* video, 7 minutes and 30 seconds, and *May you choke on a peanut,* video, 3 minutes and 50 seconds, 2006

Rami Farah, a young Syrian performer, employs various modes of address (promise, threat, curse, joke, prediction, oath, lament, praise, recollection, premonition, declaration, harangue, conciliation, and so on) in order to speak to, with, or about those who govern, about being governed, and about the governing situation. The result is a small catalogue of the different ways one can speak and act as a citizen of a state in the face of international pressures and internal stasis.

Video stills from 'Talking oneself out of a corner out of the corner of one's mouth' by Speculative Archive

I'm Syrian, lucky me!

Julia Meltzer (b. 1968) is a media artist and executive director of Clockshop, a nonprofit production company in Los Angeles. For the past ten years she has produced media projects and documentaries that deal with social issues such as police brutality and the criminal justice system. Her work has been exhibited and broadcast at venues including Creative Time's Art in the Anchorage, The New Museum of Contemporary Art, Mass MOCA, Forum Stadpark (Graz, Austria), the Next Five Minutes (Amsterdam), and select PBS stations. She received her B.A. from Brown University and her M.F.A. from Rensselaer Polytechnic Institute. She has taught video and digital media at Hampshire College and the University of California at Irvine. She is a 2004 recipient of a Rockefeller Media Arts Fellowship.

David Thorne lives and works in Los Angeles. His current projects include The Speculative Archive; the ongoing series of photo-works, *a certain interpretation based on a certain set of assumptions in order to take a certain position* (1991-present); *Boom!*, a collaboration with Austrian artist Oliver Ressler; and Scripts, a collaboration for Documenta 12 with Andrea Geyer, Sharon Hayes, Ashley Hunt, and Katya Sander. David is a 2004 recipient of a Rockefeller Media Arts Fellowship. He received his B.S. from The City University of New York in 2001, and completed his M.F.A in interdisciplinary studio at the University of California Los Angeles in 2004. Initial versions of *talking oneself out of a corner out of the corner of one's mouth* appeared in "Enemy Image," curated by Elena Sorokina at Momenta Gallery, New York, in September 2005, and as part of "I beg your pardon, or the reestablishing of cordial relations," curated by Andrea Geyer at the Vera List Center for Art and Politics, New York, October 2005.

James Pei-Mun Tsang

Hospitality
Video, 15 minutes, single channel, color, 2006

Hospitality is an experimental narrative about the so-called origins of a political subject. It is scripted by a series of conversations that occurred in Milan, Italy, during the summer of 2005. In form this video refers to a basic scenario of identity and representation: Who is speaking, and for whom? Our claims throw into relief a turning point, which designates a 'before' and 'after' to the story.

You could also talk about the gay lobby.

Video still from 'Hospitality' by James Pei-Mun Tsang

James Pei-Mun Tsang is an artist and feminist organizer who lives in Los Angeles. His recent works involve collaborations with Marriage, Pilot Television, and SubRosa. In the past two years Tsang has toured performances throughout the United States, Canada, Western Europe and Mexico. He received a bachelor's degree from the School of the Art Institute of Chicago in 2004, and he was a resident of the Fondazione Ratti in Como, Italy, in 2005.

Yates Mckee

Architecture, New Orleans, and the Specter of Ecological Justice

What is the status of experimental architectural discourse in the aftermath of Hurricane Katrina? This paper contends that unless this discourse rethinks its own relationship to what Jacques Rancière has called "the partition of the sensible," it risks lending itself to a process of mass eviction, effacing the claims of survivors in the name of greening the city's future: an aesthetically sophisticated but historically amnesiac image of "sustainability" haunted by the specter of ecological justice.

Epitomizing this risk is the book *New Orleans: Strategies for a Soft City,* the result of a studio and research project undertaken at the Harvard School of Design with the support of the Tulane Architecture Department in the 2004–5 academic year but published in December, three months into the aftermath of Hurricane Katrina. In the lead essay, entitled "The Future of New Orleans," editor Joan Busquets describes the project as "a complete reading of the spatial mechanisms at work in the transformation of the urban and territorial system of this singular deltaic space ... Specific knowledge of the city will then help to interpret the process of giving it form, but above all it may contribute to understanding the why and how behind its reconstruction."[1] As the phrase "deltaic space" suggests, the book positions New Orleans within an expanded scale of regional and ecological processes that are irreducible to—and indeed underlie—the physical structures of the city itself. Ecological expansion also means a historical deepening, a restoration of geographical and climatological memory that the city has lost. Indeed, the Katrina disaster was much more than a case of poor engineering or governmental incompetence: it resulted from an arrogant, instrumental way of conceptualizing the relationship of city and river that failed to attend to the inherently fluid topography of deltaic space. In other words, the elaborate hydrological infrastructures built during New Orleans postwar expansion provided a false sense of security, ignoring the basic ecological dynamics on which the city was originally based. This "excessive faith in the mechanisms of engineering" resulted in "permissiveness in the urbanization of very low areas, such as the Ninth ward." "Above all," writes Busquets, "the flooding of low-lying areas points to the problems caused by forgetting the city's geographical conditions that cannot be overstepped and must be part of the urban order ... The urban order must be governed by the geographical order."[2] In essence, then, the hurricane demonstrated that the pre-Katrina city was poorly adjusted to its environment and that in its destruction lie the seeds of its "sublime rebirth," giving it a chance at life based on a sustainable "dialogue" with nature rather than a defensive attempt to reverse its patterns and rhythms. Identifying and adapting to these dynamics requires historical reflection—no future without the past, in other words. The stakes of this task are significant for urbanism as a whole, especially for cities on *terra firma*, which, says Busquets, "more easily lose the memory of their relation with the location and their seminal topography."

Busquet's call for design to engage site-specific ecological memory may seem benign, but in its positing of geography as the essential foundation of urban life, Busquets unwittingly effaces the memory of those killed and displaced by the hurricane, vulnerability to which was unevenly allocated by race, class, and neighborhood.

Claiming to bypass the specific urgencies of the present, Busquets celebrates New Orleans as the subject of unitary historical trajectory. "I do not intend to speak of the difficulties that occupied during the period of emergency ... I refer to the city's urbanistic conditions and its intrinsic values. A specific climactic disaster must not entail the abandonment and discredit of one of North America's loveliest and most intriguing cities ... New Orleans can and must overcome the tragic situation created. This will call for ambition and the application of the lessons that the city and its inhabitants have learned in the past. Only in this way can a solid future be constructed in keeping with its history."[3] Busquets brackets "the emergency" of Katrina as a finite "period" in the overall life of the city, isolating it from both historically inherited dynamics of pre-storm inequality, and the ongoing emergency of the displaced survivors. By treating Katrina as essentially a problem of ecological "values," he evicts black New Orleanians from the realm of historical representation, a precondition for their permanent material eviction from the future of the city itself. Indeed, with the exception of a short, pseudo-ethnographic profile of the "King of Carnival," the studies in *New Orleans* present the city as if it were *already depopulated before the storm had even struck*.

Busquet's disturbing, though somewhat vacuous, appeal to "intrinsic urban values" is given an eco-vanguardist elaboration by Ilya Berman in her essay "Fluid Cartographies and Material Diagrams," which meditates on the inadequacy of conventional architectural procedures when confronted with the fluidity and indeterminacy of New Orleans topography. Against "the reifications of figuration" that would fix the city as a static thing, the projects outlined in *New Orleans* partake of an "evolutionary process" within design itself, one that is informed by "the deep ecological milieu from which the environment of New Orleans emerged."[4] Yet, rather than a simple organic nature, the "deep ecology" to which Berman appeals is understood in Deleuzeian terms as a "rhizomatic fluvial matrix" and thus calls for radical diagrammatic strategies capable of layering and transcoding data and landscape, time and space, form and matter in experimental ways. For Berman, the diagrammatic is "interpretative, transformative, and performative," a position she opposes to "critical claims that all is representation—(as the poststructuralists would have us believe that cultural knowledge always precedes and filters our readings of unmediated matter)." Berman thus positions herself as a species of architectural activist, deploying both scientific and formal rigor to "disrupt habitual modes of envisioning the real" that "resist the ease of accessibility that accompanies images intended for simple consumption."[5]

Yet Berman's dismissal of "representation" should disturb us—rather than an epistemological question of "cultural filters," so-called poststructuralism concerns the unforeseeably mediated network of discourses, practices, institutions, and histories that mark our thinking and acting and implicate us, unevenly, in the world with others. "Representation" signals as an ethico-political attention to the exclusions that govern the conditions of speech and response, the limits to who or what can appear at a given conjuncture. While motivated by a desire for justice, poststructuralism demands that we remain vigilant about our complicity in violence, even when engaged in the most conscientious of radical aesthetic and political endeavors. These are questions that *New Orleans,* despite its vanguardist vocabulary of vectors, fields, and rhizomes, utterly fails to ask, and so ends up defining the city as "a floating sponge, a semi-stable ecosystem supported by an intricately entangled biomorphic fabric, a woven living matrix." This definition is offered as "a backdrop to the current and future debates that will govern the rebuilding of New Orleans. And without this expansive reenvisioning of what we believe to know and understand about this place we will never produce anything other than the reinstantiation of habitual typological realities and mute development which we already know are unsustainable within this environment."[6] It is important to note that Berman conceives of the forces against which the eco-vanguard positions itself in primarily aesthetico-formal terms—insofar as they are maladjusted to the true biomorphological coordinates of the city, the "habitual typologies" and "mute development" that would make New Orleans unsustainable, rather than, say, the uneven allocation of environmental risk, spatial resources, and political power.

In its rhetoric of biomorphism, which effaces the *biopolitics* of Katrina, *New Orleans* unwittingly lends itself to the ethnic and class cleansing of redevelopment elites such as Joe Canizaro, a well-connected real estate mogul appointed by the mayor to chair the urban planning committee of the Bring Back New Orleans Commission, who notoriously remarked, "As a practical matter these poor folks don't have the resources to go back to our city just like they didn't have the resources to get out of our city. So we won't get all those folks back. That's just a fact."[7] Significantly, Canizaro is the former head of the Urban Land Institute (ULI), the chief think tank and advocacy group of the New Urbanism, the design philosophy embodied by the planned community of Seaside, Florida. In its aesthetically traditionalist and suspiciously communitarian vision of the revitalized city, the New Urbanism is typically the scourge of vanguard design discourse, the other against which advanced, critical practice defines itself.

This position was explicitly taken in the March edition of *Artforum,* which featured a collection of "visionary" proposals by American and Dutch designers brought together by the dean of Tulane Architecture School Reed Kroloff, and Aaron Betsky, curator at the National Architecture Institute in Rotterdam.

Kroloff begins his introduction to the projects with a firsthand description of walking through the ruined landscape of an unspecified New Orleans neighborhood, which he characterizes as "spooky," "ghostly," and "almost dead," especially at night. "There's nothing out there. No lights. No people. No police, no sound, no horizon, no hope."[8] Yet the pathos of this wasted, indeed terrifying landscape provides the background against which he can pose the revitalizing vocation of architecture. Accepting that "New Orleans is going to be a mess for a long time," he writes, "this city needs bright visions to contrast with the bleak present that surrounds us . . . We need inspiration and innovation, glimpses into a promising and expressive future."

This visionary impulse is resolutely opposed to the New Urbanists, "who would have us believe our only future resides in the past" and who offer a "candy-coated dream-version" of the city that Kroloff denounces as "quaint, predictable and market friendly." But despite the alarming success of the "New Urbanist Svengalis," "no one has offered an alternative to their toothache of a future ... the projects you see here inaugurate an important dialogue. They bring fresh new vision to a city waiting to hear that its greatest days are not behind it, that it has an architectural future that will stride confidently beyond its past."

Kroloff's raising the alarm about New Urbanism is important: it is indeed urgent to interrogate, especially as it is currently functioning in the discourses of New Orleans reconstruction. But in so doing it is crucial for us to think critically about why and in which ways we do so, lest we reproduce the worst aspects of the very thing critical architecture would claim to oppose.

The stakes of this criticality—or lack thereof—become evident in Aaron Betsky's article, which meditates on how architecture might contribute to the reenvisioning and reconstruction of the city.[9] Unlike *New Orleans*, Betsky frames his remarks with an explicit criticism of the politico-economic dynamics of the city, writing, "The situation in New Orleans is only an extreme instance of the quandary in which arch in general finds itself—when the economic realities imposed on us by relentless market forces compel the proliferation of nonplaces leached of any individual or social meaning or coherence, how is architecture to respond?" Yet, echoing Ilya Berman's claims to resist "habitual typological patterns" and Roof's denunciation of "the sugar-coated future" offered by New Urbanism, Betsky's main objection to "market forces" appears to be that it threatens to reduce the aesthetic and spiritual qualities of urban place—it is against this alienating privation of "meaning" that architecture finds its specific competence. Betsky acknowledges the importance of housing, but writes that "the provision of adequate dwelling for the displaced is not an activity in which architecture can play a role beyond making sure the houses are safe and more or less aesthetically pleasing. Where, how much, at what price, and who will live there is currently being decided by politicians and no doubt real-estate interests." While Betsky's last point is in one sense true, in the name of realism he cynically takes the domination of the housing discussion by elites for granted, narrowly framing it as an unsavory technical part of the reconstruction process from which advanced architecture should be content to keep a distance. Rather than enter into the fractious, interested realm of politics, which he defines in advance as encompassing only professional politicians rather than citizens, architecture should contribute its efforts to a higher end—namely, remaking the architectural image and landscape ecology of the city itself. Betsky complains that "no one seems to be asking why anybody would return to New Orleans in the first place. Every city needs its unique selling points and needs to attract investment. Old New Orleans was in decline. Katrina turned that gradual decay into catastrophe. Why *would* anyone come back?" Not unlike Busquets, Betsky sees the disaster as an opportunity for urban ecological rebirth, and he proceeds unquestioningly to reiterate the claim that "New Orleans is now clearly, in all likelihood irrevocably, one of the worlds shrinking cities ... What is interesting is the fact that nature is coming back in many of these areas ... The vast voids left by deindustrialization and depopulation are turning back into forest and field ... As cities still suburbanize, nature is returning into the inner city, and it can draw people back to these burned out cores. At the same time, old cities still retain legacies of past achievement ... and they need to retain historic character to become attractive again because of their density and their closeness to cultural amenities. And herein lie the elements for the rebirth of cities: new nature, old culture, and strong communities ... We believe these elements can also help New Orleans to transform itself into a successful Newer Orleans—a smaller, more compact, and more beautiful city that would use its natural setting and cultural heritage to enhance viable neighborhoods and attract both new businesses and new residents ... [For the exhibition *Newer Orleans: A Shared Space*] We asked firms to address the issues of how architecture could facilitate community, create an urban icon to house the city's cultural patrimony, and provide a way of connecting the city back to its landscape."

Now community, cultural heritage, and landscape are terms that no one can simply oppose. The problem is that Betsky, while obviously having liberal tendencies,[10] takes for granted that the meanings of these principles are universally shared, disavowing them as sites of conflict over what Rancière calls the "partition of the sensible": the limits of what can be said, seen, heard, and recalled in a given sociopolitical configuration, and the resulting "parts" different social agents are assigned—including the poor, or the "part with no part."[11] Rancière's concept enables to understand the stakes of the "right to return" declared by groups such as the ACORN Katrina Survivors; this right unsettles the self-evidence of both political and physical territory, suggesting that the future of spaces is inextricably bound up with the conflicting ways in which their histories are marked, represented, and interpreted.[12] Inhabiting and displacing the ubiquitous mantra about the dependence of the urban future on a sense of the past, the right to return challenges Betsky's narrow demarcation of the politics of housing and his uncritical acceptance of the "shrinking cities" narrative, which in fact bears a disturbing affinity with the class-cleansing discourse of figures such as Canizaro and the self-fulfilling forecast by the Rand Corporation in April that half of New Orleans's pre-storm diaspora will in fact not return to the city.[13] Needless to say, in questioning such a position one should not be glib about the massive obstacles facing the return of displaced people, or the serious ecological and infrastructural issues to be dealt with in low-lying areas of the city. From the perspective of ecological justice however, the point is to recognize these as realms of political dispute and negotiation, rather than submit to them as demographic inevitabilities or as matters of sheer technical expertise to which designers should defer. Yet this is precisely what Betsky does, which permits him to conclude his essay thus: "These projects seek to house a sense of community, attract attention and activity, and make the landscape visible. They propose a shared space, both physical and mental, around which the city could organize itself in a meaningful manner. And in so doing, they not only suggest an architecture for a newer Orleans but also a potential way for making all of us at home in an increasingly alien world."[14] Alluding to the etymological tie that links the Greek *oikos* to the figure of the household, Betsky urges the "housing" of urban community, but only as an eco-phenomenological horizon rather than as a *political* demand for the right to return and its corollary, a "Right to Housing."[15] Betsky's liberal ideal of "new" city properly at home with itself unwittingly commits an act of domestic violence, recalling Mark Wigley's remark apropos of Heidegger: "The house of metaphysics represses the violence that makes it possible."[16] Confronted with the often sinister appeals of deep-ecological rhetoric, the task of radical architecture—if there is such a thing[17]—would thus be to engage the specific claims, activities, and aspirations of displaced people struggling to "come home" to New Orleans while keeping watch over their own discipline's proclivity for both domestication and eviction.

1. "The Future of New Orleans: Summary of the New Orleans Studio and Consideration After Katrina," in *New Orleans: Strategies for a Soft City,* ed. J. Busquets and F. Correa (Cambridge, Mass.: Harvard University School of Design, 2006), 13.
2. Ibid., 16.
3. Ibid. p. 13.
4. Ilya Berman, "Fluid Cartographies and Material Diagrams," in *New Orleans*, 30.
5. Ibid., 29.
6. Ibid., 34.
7. Quoted in Mike Davis, "Who Is Killing New Orleans?" *The Nation,* 10 April 2006 (http://www.thenation.com/doc/20060410/davis).
8. Reed Kroloff, "A Newer Orleans: A Shared Space," *Artforum* (March 2006): xx.
9. Aaron Betsky, "Six Proposals," *Artforum* (March 2006): xx.
10. For an extended class critique of liberal social scientists' response to the disaster, see Adolph Reed and Stephen Steinberg, "Liberal Bad Faith in the Wake of Hurricane Katrina," http://www.zmag.org/content/showarticle.cfm?ItemID = 10205.
11. See Jacques Rancière, *The Politics of Aesthetics*, trans. Gabrielle Rockhill (London: Continuum, 2004).
12. See http://www.acorn.org/index.php?id = 9703.
13. See Davis, "Who's Killing New Orleans?".
14. Betsky, "Six Proposals", xx.
15. Rachel G. Bratt et al., *A Right to Housing: Foundations for a New Social Agenda* (Philadelphia: Temple University Press, 2006).
16. "The Domestication of the House," in *The Architecture of Deconstruction: Derrida's Haunt* (Cambridge, Mass.: MIT Press, 1997) 97–121.
17. Manfredo Tafuri famously admonished that, under capitalism, there can be no "radical architecture" but only a class critique of "architectural ideology" and its "hopes in design." Fredric Jameson has revised Tafuri's pessimistic position, arguing for a Gramscian sense of counterhegemonic "enclaves" tactically operating within the capitalist city. See "Architecture and the Critique of Ideology" in *Ideologies of Theory 1* (Minneapolis: University of Minnesota, 1985), xx. Jameson's point is pertinent to the activities of the Common Ground collective (www.commongroundreleif.org), which has coordinated large groups of residents and volunteers to assist in the gutting and renovation of damaged homes in the lower Ninth Ward and other devastated neighborhoods at risk of being razed unless their dispersed communities can prove their long-term "viability." Without diminishing the importance of these efforts, it seems important for architects not to romanticize them as figures of bottom-up spontaneity, which could result in detracting attention from the longer-term, larger-scale constraints, mediations, uncertainties, and inequalities that mark the reconstruction environment in which groups such as Common Ground and ACORN are struggling to operate.

Yates McKee is a writer, critic and Ph.D. student in the Department of Art History, Columbia University. His current project is entitled "Art and the Ends of Environmentalism: From Biosphere to the Right to Survival." He co-curated the exhibition "Empire/State" at the Whitney ISP and coordinated the recent 16Beaver event "8 short talks on bio-art, bio-tech, bio-politics" at MIT's Center for Advanced Visual Studies. He has also written texts engaged with works by Alia Hasan-Khan, Allora & Calzadilla, Jesal Kapadia and Thorne & Ressler.

RETHINKING MARXISM   VOLUME 18   NUMBER 4   (OCTOBER 2006)

From Imperialism to Transnational Capitalism: The Venice Biennial as a "Transitional Conjuncture"

Yahya M. Madra

This essay offers a critical review of the 51st Venice Biennial (12 June–6 November 2005), situating it in the context of the recent history of the Venice Biennial. The review identifies a dual institutional structure (national pavilions and international survey shows) in the Venice Biennial, and argues that this constitutes a "transitional conjuncture" overdetermined by the radicalization and pluralization of art practices (performances, site-specific installations, etc.), the privatization of art funding in the form of corporate sponsorship, and the global proliferation and consolidation of the institutional form of the biennial—biannual survey exhibitions of transnational art practices. The review argues that, while a number of artists and curators have succeeded in the past and in this year's edition in producing self-reflective and acutely critical art works in relation to the older structure of the Venice Biennial where art was displayed and appropriated in national pavilions, the two survey exhibitions of the 2005 edition (curated by Rosa Martínez and María de Corral) have failed to reflect critically upon the new, corporate-sponsored institutional form of the biennial that the Venice Biennial is moving toward.

Key Words: 51st Venice Biennial, Culture Industry, Institutional Critique, Critical Art Practices, Spectacle as a Commodity, Value of Art

The very architectural forms that populate the Giardini of the Venice Biennial, the main garden where the permanent national pavilions are located, inadvertently reveal the traces of the overdetermined history of this oldest of all biennials. The neoclassical splendor of the buildings of the *fin-de-siècle* imperial powers such as Great Britain, France, Germany (rebuilt in the 1930s), and Italy, the modernist slickness of the pavilions of the established nation-states of the proverbial North —Sweden and Norway, Australia, Spain, and Japan and, of course, the late imperial Palladian style of the U.S. pavilion (built in the 1930s) make it crystal clear, at least for this fascinated viewer, that there is indeed a geopolitically constituted pecking order in the world of art. Any nation-state that does not have a permanent pavilion, yet wishes to participate in the Biennial (e.g., Turkey, Afghanistan, Iran, Central Asian Republics, Armenia, Wales, India), has to rent a space in the city, most probably in one of the overpriced empty palazzos that are struggling to stay afloat (in most cases literally) in a state of decrepitude.

ISSN 0893-5696 print/1475-8059 online/06/040525-13
© 2006 Association for Economic and Social Analysis
DOI: 10.1080/08935690600901194

Routledge
Taylor & Francis Group

In this sense, the Biennial, inaugurated in 1895 by the Venice City Council, is marked in its very architectural structure by the inequalities of the colonialist world order that has funded and continues to fund the art displayed in these pavilions. In the 51st edition of the Venice Biennial (12 June–6 November 2005) there were seventy national pavilions (a record number), but only thirty of them were inside the Giardini. It is not difficult to interpret the not-at-all invisible garden fence that delineates the borders of the Giardini as the border that separates the North from the South, the core from the periphery. Indeed, in the nerve-wracking humidity of Venice, the temptation to be a postcolonial critic is strong.

An Uneven Development in Venice

Starting with the mid-1960s, however, perhaps as a consequence of the general radicalization of the art scene, the Biennial has begun to go through an important transformation. When Robert Rauschenberg received the Grand Prize in Venice in 1964, this meant for many that the art establishment had begun to take pop art seriously. The 1968 edition was marked by social uprisings; the 1972 edition was when Diane Arbus represented the United States; the 1974 edition was dedicated to Chile, in opposition to Pinochet's coup d'état; the 1976 edition was the first time Joseph Beuys represented Germany; the 1980 edition was when Achille Bonito Oliva and the late Harald Szeemann co-curated the Aperto '80, an international group show that featured emerging and young artists. In the 1980s and especially the 1990s, the center of gravity of the Biennial shifted from the national pavilions to group exhibitions curated by internationally acknowledged curators including, among others, Oliva (1993), Jean Clair (1995), Germano Celant (1997), Szeemann (1999 and 2001), and Francesco Bonami (2003). (And let us note in passing what we have learned from the Guerrilla Girls (fig. 1), that this curatorial post has indeed been, up until this last edition, a male privilege.) Each curator, without doubt, would invite the group of artists that he works with. And as the curatorial practice has become increasingly transnational over this period, the contrast between these group exhibitions that feature artists from an increasingly transnational pool and the national pavilions that tend to appropriate their artists as the "representatives" of the nation-state has become more and more apparent.

In a sense, therefore, the Venice Biennial has been for the last two decades and is still going through an uneven, incomplete, contradictory—in short, overdetermined—transition from one *mode of appropriation of art* to another. By the appropriation of art I mean the *performative act of situating, understanding, making sense, and making use of art*. For instance, in the earlier yet still perpetuating nation-state/imperial mode, the art product was cast as a sublimated object that functions as *the representative of the national identity*. In other words, the art was appropriated by first the imperialist nation-states and then, in the postcolonial era, by the emerging nation-states of the global South as a symbol of prestige, refined taste, civilization, development, and being modern.

In contrast, the emerging new mode is decidedly a transnational one and constituted by a rather contradictory set of conditions. On the one hand, as noted

Figure 1   Guerrilla Girls, *Where are the women artists of Venice? Underneath the men*. The Arsenale, Venice, 2005. Photo by author.

earlier, there is the radicalization of the art scene. In the past three decades, art practices that are critical not only in terms of the themes that they explore (e.g., questions of identity, matters of social justice and exclusion) but also in terms of the formal aspects of art practice have gained an international standing. For instance, happenings, multimedia performances, site-specific installations, and other inter-disciplinary strategies that have been adopted by artists, in part, in order to resist the appropriation of art not only by the art market but also by the nation-state, have become more and more prominent.

Yet, on the other hand, this radicalization of art practice has been accompanied by a transition in the financing and funding of art. Perhaps as a by-product of the global hegemony of neoliberal economic policies, there is a secular decline in the capacity and willingness of nation-states to finance and fund art. Countering this waning of the public funding of art has been the growing importance of the institution of "corporate sponsorship." In fact, despite all the revolutionary intentions of the emerging critical art practice, art remains a source of prestige for its patrons, albeit different ones. It would probably be stating the obvious to remind the reader that the new patrons are the transnational corporations.

Without doubt, this dual transition (the simultaneous radicalization of art practice and the corporatization of art funding) needed a new institutional form. As it has become impossible to sell art as a "sublimated" object—the very premise of critical art practices has been to deconstruct the object-hood of art—the need for new institutional *forms*, that would substitute for the art galleries and auctions where art used to be exchanged, has become more and more urgent. I believe that the institution of the biennial is one such *form*.

Let us be empirical for a moment. The number of biennials has increased exponentially in the past three decades. Here are the names of a subset of biennials and the years that they were launched: Sydney (1973), Havana (1984), Istanbul (1987), Sharjah, United Arab Emirates (1993), Johannesburg (1995), Kwangju, Korea (1995), Berlin (1998), Tirana (2001), Moscow (2005). Biennials serve several mutually reinforcing functions. First, they offer biannual surveys of international art practice for the benefit of viewers from the region. They serve, in part, an educational function for the local audiences, for they nurture an appreciation of the "transnational standards" of aesthetic practices. It is important to emphasize, however, that it is in and through these biennials that these "transnational standards" are being set and produced. In this sense, the biennials serve a double purpose. They are simultaneously the sites where transnational standards are being imposed on the local art scenes *and* the portals of subversion where the host cities and their regional hinterlands can insert their own discourses into the transnational conversation.[1] Second, as they have become sites where the practice of the selected artists is valorized (i.e., the economic value of the art practice is *sociosymbolically produced*), they fulfill the economic role of the art market. Third, they contribute

---

1. Readers of an earlier draft noted the negative tone of the analysis of biennials offered in this essay. Admittedly this essay articulates very little as to the radical potential offered by the emerging system of transnational biennials. Let me use this opportunity to note that it would be wrong to argue that the emerging institutional form of biennials qua spectacle-commodity necessarily entails the *cooptation* of contemporary art practices. First of all, we now know that it is possible to produce commodities without reverting to a capitalistic (i.e., exploitative) form of production and appropriation of surplus. It is possible to produce, for instance, "communist" commodities. Second, the transnational and decentered form of the biennial system somewhat paradoxically enables (or gives the opportunity to) the semiperipheries to insert their own discourses into the transnational conversation thus far dominated/dictated by the core (New York, Los Angeles, London, Paris, Berlin, etc.). Whether this opportunity has so far been realized by the semiperiphery is another question. On the multicenteredness of globalization, see Dirlik (2000).

to the cultural "capital" of the city. And in this third function, they constitute a moment in a broader tendency towards the "festivalization" of arts.

By festivalization, I refer to the global circulation of art through international festivals. For instance, the foundation that produces the Venice Biennial also produces a prestigious film festival and an architecture biennial. The foundation that produces the Istanbul Biennial also produces annual festivals for classical music, jazz/pop, theater, and film. Inevitably, the Venice Biennial itself is also affected by this process and is forced to adopt its structure to the rapidly standardizing organizational form of the biennials. According to this structure, biennials are sponsored by a number of transnational corporations, their local subsidiaries, and the city government; are organized by one or two main internationally renowned curators, preferably well connected with an established network of artists as well as sponsors; and feature forty to sixty artists chosen according to a somewhat broad yet predetermined theme.

It is important to explore, if only briefly, the extent to which this uncanny alliance between radical art practices and transnational corporations is an effect of a conjunctural balance of forces or an inherent shortcoming of the analyses of capitalism that informed the postwar radicalization of art practices. While the period after World War II was when radical art practices really took off, the story can easily begin at an earlier moment—for instance, at that revolutionary moment in 1917 (!) when Marcel Duchamp took a urinal, signed it, and displayed it as an art object. Since then, it has become impossible to conceive of art outside the "institutional" context (galleries, museums, art journals, art critics, collectors, sponsors, etc.) that sociosymbolically produces the meaning as well as the value of the art object (Ruccio, Graham, and Amariglio 1997). As they became increasingly wary of producing art *objects* that can be easily folded into the circuit of commodity exchange, critical artists began to invent and develop strategies that question, subvert, and resist the commodification of art. In the 1960s and 1970s, if Andy Warhol, down at the Factory working hard to erase the difference between the art *object* and the commodity, was at one end of the spectrum of possible strategies of subversion, at the other end there was Beuys, a modern shaman sweeping the streets after political demonstrations and offering this public service as a gift to the community. In fact, just as the "private goods" that populate Warhol's silkscreens are metonyms of the market-centered model of American capitalism that Warhol was critical of, the "public goods" that Beuys performed were metonyms of the state-centered model of German capitalism.

Yet, in opposition to this critical vector that radically changed art practice was the mounting hegemony of what Theodor Adorno (1991) called the "culture industry." Adorno's concept of culture industry relies upon Marx's simple idea that, under capitalism, what is important for the capitalist is the *form* of commodity and not the commodity as such. In this sense, capitalism is indeed an "abstraction machine" that can potentially treat anything and everything as a commodity, including performances and site-specific installations. In terms of the political economy of contemporary art, this means that even a critical art practice can have market value, perhaps not as an *object* that can be bought and sold by collectors but as a *spectacle* produced by art schools, museums, journals, critics, curators, and public relations experts, through

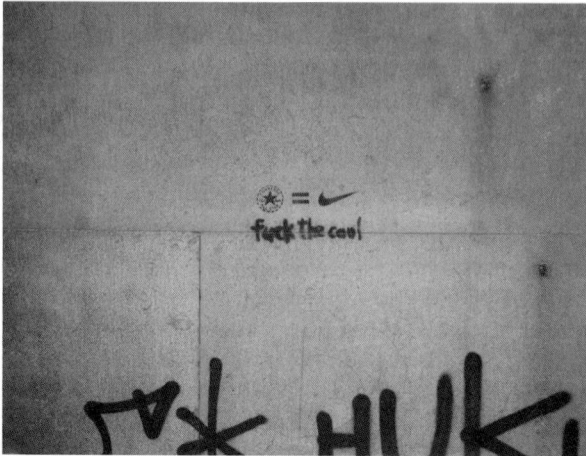

Figure 2 A Situationist graffiti from the streets of Venice, June 2005. Photo by author.

biennials, themed exhibitions, and retrospectives sponsored by transnational corporations and consumed by the tourists/viewers as these shows travel the globe from one city to another—in short, a *spectacle* produced by an entire culture industry (see fig. 2).[2]

Juxtaposing an artist who produces colorful, always already sold out, and ultimately decorative *objects* (Thomas Scheibitz) with an artist who categorically rejects producing material objects and who stages *performances* that cannot be photographically recorded (Tino Sehgal), the German pavilion (curated by Julian Heynen) for the 2005 Venice Biennial concretized the inherent limitations of radical art practices in devising sustainable strategies for resisting commodification. When viewers entered the pavilion, if the first things they *saw* were the modern kitsch objects of Scheibitz, the first thing they *heard* was a small chorus singing, "Oh! It's so contemporary, contemporary, contemporary!" The latter, of course, was a part of the "immaterial" art-work that Sehgal staged for the visitors, and it was a perpetually looping dance-song routine performed by local actors dressed in white and black as museum guards. After a moment of surprise, the sarcasm of the song and its apparent ridicule of Scheibitz's objects seduced this viewer into thinking that Sehgal is a part of the tradition that criticizes the commodification of art.

This impression was further encouraged in an antechamber of the pavilion where another band of actors dressed like guards invited one to have a conversation on "market economics" promising, in exchange (!), a refund of the admission price for the Giardini. Yet, the conversation between the artist and the German philosopher Peter Sloterdijk, published in the edition of the German weekly *Die Zeit* (24/2005) that came out on the weekend of the opening week of the show, compelled me

2. On the notion of spectacle, the classic reference is Guy Debord's *The Society of the Spectacle* (1995). For a fine theoretical and political assessment of Situationism, see MacDonald (1995).

to reconsider my judgment (http://www.zeit.de/2005/24/Sehgal_2fSloterdijk). Perhaps being true to the spirit of his earlier training as a political economist, Sehgal insists that his work is not a critique of the commodity form and that he wishes to sell his works. Rather, he argues, he is producing, just like the contemporary culture industry, "an organization of subjectivity." The example he uses to explain the formal structure of what he calls "organization of subjectivity" is the case of a mobile phone company that sells a new cellphone every other season by simply changing its "look."

Without doubt, Sehgal's analysis of the logic of the commodity form is very accurate and it was his work and definitely not Scheibitz's modern kitsch that made the Germany pavilion interesting. The very juxtaposition of the two works clarifies for us that the commodity has never been, even in the colonial/imperial era, simply an object, but that it has always been an "organization of subjectivity." To put it differently, Sehgal's cynical *yet* honest willingness to "sell" his performance pieces (Yes, they can be sold!) makes it possible to see that the uncanny alliance between the transnational corporations and radical art practices was bound to happen sooner or later.

The Crisis of National Pavilions

At least for a couple decades now, the Venice Biennial has been going through an uneven and undoubtedly incomplete transition from a "nation-state/imperial" mode of appropriating art to a new "transnational" mode. Yet, this emerging transnational mode is not simply replacing the earlier national mode. The newer editions of the Biennial have included both types of exhibitions, and there is indeed an "exchange," a political negotiation between the two modes, that is worth discussing in some detail. For instance, at the 2005 edition, a number of national pavilions featured small-sized group exhibitions with artists who could simply be living and working in that country without being a citizen, who could be living in diaspora, or who could entertain an even more ambiguous relationship to the country that he or she is supposed to be representing. As one example, Hussein Chalayan, who was featured in the national pavilion of Turkey (curated by Beral Madra), is neither a citizen of the Republic of Turkey nor does he live there; he is a Cypriot of Turkish ethnicity who lives and works in London.[3]

Moreover, it would be equally incorrect to claim that only national pavilions featured art qua sublime objects while the "transnational" group exhibitions featured only the new critical art practices. In "The Experience of Art," one of the two main international group shows of the 51st Biennial, among the more conservative works qua sublimated, art market–friendly objects, one could mention

3. Let me note that Chalayan's past works have been critical of the traumatic partitioning of the island of Cyprus as a result of the 1974 occupation of its northern half by the Turkish military, and subsequently, by the settlers from Anatolia ushered forth by the Turkish government. To add an additional layer of contradiction to this particular case, let me also note that among the sponsors of the Pavilion of Turkey was Turquality, a private-public public relations project that aims to upgrade Turkey's image as a quality-brand textile and clothing producer!

Francis Bacon's paintings, Rachel Whiteread's plaster cast of the void of a staircase, and Thomas Schütte's prize-winning shiny silver voluptuous female torso. Without doubt, since the group exhibitions usually survey works that have already received a "pass" from the art establishment, they are almost always more in tune with the mainstream of contemporary art practices. National pavilions, however, especially when they do not play the game in a savvy manner, cannot help but appear anachronistic. (Consider, for instance, the case of the Egyptian pavilion.)

The crisis of national pavilions, however, is much deeper; playing it savvy is becoming increasingly less effective in keeping this crisis under control. An important work that encircled this transitional conjuncture through the heavy-handed yet acute language of "institutional critique" was offered by none other than Hans Haacke when he represented Germany at the 1993 edition of the Biennial.[4] His work was an intervention to the neoclassical building of the German pavilion (renovated after 1938 under the auspices of Hitler), not only to its monumental architectural form, but also to its institutional function as a complicit mo(nu)ment of the fascist social formation that produced it, both physically and sociosymbolically. Greeted outside with a sculptural detail of an enlarged plaster replica German Mark coin on the pediment of the building, the viewer, once inside, was confronted with a Protestant white cathedral with a capitalized GERMANIA in the apse and an entirely shattered floor. By encircling the institutional as well as the aesthetic complicity of the very concept of the national pavilion, Haacke was "remarking" his own complicity, his function as the artist who was representing Germany, along with the video artist Nam June Paik, in Venice 1993.

In the 2003 edition of the Biennial, Santiago Sierra, an artist who was born in Spain but who lives and works in Mexico, sealed off the Spanish pavilion to everyone except those who had a Spanish passport. While it is quite plausible to read Sierra's stratagem as a critique of the ideology of "Fortress Europe," it would be a mistake to neglect its strong critique of the institution of the national pavilion. By reducing the sublimated pavilion that is supposed to harbor precious art objects into what it really is—a slice of national territory—Sierra was offering his variation on the theme that Haacke began to explore back in 1993.

The 2005 biennial also had its share of subversions of the national pavilions. The artist Daniel Knorr chose to leave the Romanian pavilion empty, deliberately exposing the traces of past exhibitions. Entitled *European Influenza*, the work was an "invisible artwork," a minimalist intervention that exposed the building, the institution, and its performative function in eliciting a concrete identity that would fill its void (fig. 3). Rather than a concrete artwork qua an imaginary object, we were offered a small pocketbook-sized reader (edited by the commissioner/curator Marius Babias) packed with critical texts written by mostly Eastern European art critics, curators, philosophers, and so on. In 1993, Haacke achieved a critical analysis of the earlier nation-state/imperialist mode of the Biennial by adding to the building, by revealing its institutional complicity, its formal and aesthetic readiness to be a part of the fascist machine. In contrast, Knorr's act of subtraction may be read as a

---

4. For useful discussions of "institutional critique," see Alberro (1997) and Fraser (2005).

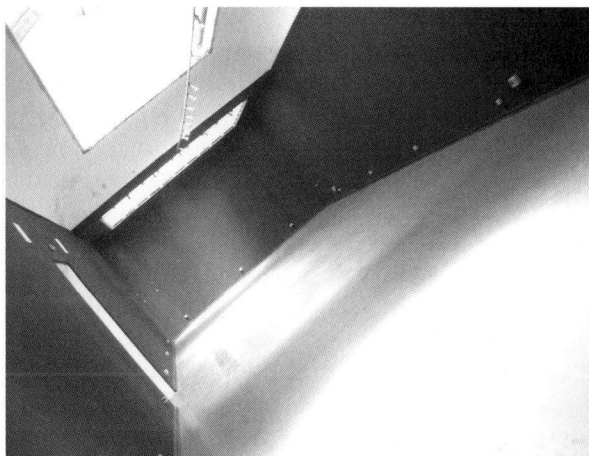

Figure 3   Daniel Knorr, *European Influenza*. The Pavilion of Romania, 2005. Photo by author.

commentary on the emerging internationalist mode that erases the nation-state as a relevant category and the very questions of identity that Romania and other Eastern European nation-states are trying to answer in their recent or impending subsumption under the European Union. The title, *European Influenza*, elicits this interpretation. Yet it also referenced, at least for this viewer, another epidemic: the cholera epidemic that took the life of one Gustave von Aschenbach in Thomas Mann's *Death in Venice*. The reader may recall that that epidemic, like all epidemics, was supposed to originate in a hallucinated "Far East." Knorr's *European Influenza* turns this Orientalist fantasy inside out and designates Europe as the origin of the epidemic.

To put it differently, if, in 1993, Haacke could not bring himself to "represent" Germany without engaging with the institutional and architectural history of the national pavilion, in 2005, Knorr must have felt that it had become simply *impossible* to "represent" Romania. The very existence of the "thing" that the signifier "Romania" is supposed to represent has itself come into question as this country has acceded to the European Union. In short, the transition within the Venice Biennial is itself overdetermined by the geopolitical changes that constitute its context. Yet, it is also important to note that the earlier form persists, that the national pavilions still exist, and that the artists representing their countries are still representing them even as, or perhaps precisely because, they criticize them.

"Bienvenuti alla Biennale Feminista!"

If the visitor did not learn in advance that this was the first edition ever of the Venice Biennial that featured not one but two major international group exhibitions curated by woman curators (Rosa Martínez and María de Corral), she would do so upon her arrival at the exhibition in the Arsenale, the old shipyard of Venice. "Always a little further," curated by Martínez, greeted the viewer with two giant billboard posters designed by the Guerrilla Girls. While one of them was welcoming (*Bienvenuti alla Biennale Feminista!*), the other posed a rhetorical question only to answer it immediately: *Where are the women artists of Venice? Underneath the men.* This question and answer were typeset in bold over the famous still from Federico Fellini's *La Dolce Vita* (1961) featuring a beastly Marcello Mastroianni riding a woman (fig. 1). From these performative as well as informative posters, one learns not only that the percentage of women artists in the first biennial in 1895 was 2.4 percent, but also that not much had changed a century later, in 1995 (9 percent)!

Martínez's selection did indeed have a feminist tone, but it was far from exclusively feminist. Rather, it was an exhibition that politicized "identity" in general. As the viewer moved from one hall of the Corderie (a beautiful and endlessly stretching rope factory within the Arsenale) to another, the title of the exhibition started to make sense. In work after work, one saw the same incessant and self-reflective mode of questioning being repeated always in a new context; each work circled around a particular question of identity, each work questioned "identity," each work questioned its own identity, and so on.

Since this was supposed to be the feminist Biennial, let me begin by highlighting some of the more interesting feminist works (or works by feminist artists) in the group exhibition curated by Martínez. In the very first hall, literally encircled by the more familiar Guerrilla Girls billboards, was a huge, used condom–shaped chandelier made out of hundreds of tampons by Joana Vasconcelos (fig. 4). In the next hall, Turkish opera singer the late Semiha Berksoy's expressionist/cubist paintings depicting women and cats preceded Runa Islam's video projection which documented a women dropping and breaking fine pottery in slow motion. Walk on two more halls and Mona Hatoum's $-/+$, a minimalist, circular sand pool simultaneously smoothed and raked by rotating 180 degrees stretched arms, distilled the endless cycle of household labor into a formula. In the next hall on the left was a video by Regina José Galindo featuring a woman washing her feet in a blood-red liquid. In the last hall of the building, after a series of dark rooms featuring one video installation after another, the viewer was sent out of the building with a video work by the Spanish performance artist Pilar Albarracín. In the video, Albarracín, dressed up in a chic yellow coat and fashionable dark sunglasses, not unlike a woman character from a Buñuel or Almodovar movie, rushes through the streets of Madrid with a small brass section following and harassing her by incessantly playing "Viva España."

Yet, it would be unfair to essentialize (even if for strategic reasons) the strong presence of feminist themes at the expense of others. For instance, Brazilian artist Rivane Neuenschwander's manipulated Olivetti typewriters that can only be useful today as objects of art; Ukrainian Oleg Kulik's long "documentary" of his journey into "deep" Siberia; Palestinian artist Emily Jacir's juxtaposition of mundane scenes from Ramallah and New York (hairdressers, offices, grocery stores, etc.); Albanian artist Adrian Paci's short video featuring, presumably, Albanian workers who start up generator motors only to turn their low-dimmed lights on; and Turkish artist Bülent Şangar's overflowing public buses—all are works of art that take as their subject the marginalized other of the liberal democratic capitalist mainstream.

In short, many of the works had a strong political accent, and not only a feminist one at that. Yet, at the same time, the exhibition as a whole felt "reformist,"

Figure 4   Joana Vasconcelos, *The Bride*, 2001. The image is from the Arsenale, Venice, 2005. Photo by author.

formulaic, and sterile. In other words, even Guerrilla Girls' performative appropriation of the exhibition as a concerted feminist effort failed to give an edge to "Always a little further."

This "reformist" tone was even more accentuated in the other major survey exhibition of the Biennial. "The Experience of Art," curated by María de Corral, took place in the Italian pavilion, which is located inside the main Garden. The works included here were from South African artists William Kentridge, Marlene Dumas, Candice Breitz, and Robin Rhode; German artists Thomas Ruff and Thomas Schütte; British artists Francis Bacon, Rachel Whiteread, and Mark Wallinger; and North American stars like Jenny Holzer, Barbara Kruger, Bruce Nauman, Dan Graham, and Stan Douglas. Several of these left a mark: Ruff's overenlarged jpeg thumbnail images, Dumas's portrait depicting the ecstasy of death, and Breitz's video installation that restaged well-known family dramas between father and son and mother and daughter (in two separate dark screening rooms) through a perfect pitch sampling and sequencing of signature sound-images of Hollywood stars. Also worth a mention were works by the Venetian Monica Bonvinici (a machine-sound-gun hanging down from the ceiling and intermittently "shooting" at unsuspecting visitors), the

Argentinian Jorge Macchi (a forest made out of compressed phonebooks), and the Cuban Tania Bruguera (an elevated corridor covered with used teabags and little video screens embedded within them).

If, however, I call these two exhibitions "reformist," it is certainly not because the works selected were not radical enough or failed to include in their analysis a critique of various forms of social injustice or exclusion. In fact, in the Arsenale exhibition, both the sound installation by Spanish artist Santiago Sierra and the documentary banners by Dutch architect Rem Koolhaas did furnish the visitors with a generous amount of information regarding the political economy of the Venice Biennial and the contemporary art system, respectively. In fact, these exhibitions were "reformist" not only *despite* but also *because of* the political nature of each and every work.

Let me try to be more explicit. The term "reformism" for me designates the tendency to accept the very formal coordinates of an institution and to try to navigate within it. In this sense, these exhibitions were reformist precisely because they naturalized/reified the very institutional form of the biennials, a form that turns the radical art practices gathered therein into a *spectacle* that has no relation to their broader context—to the social formation within which they are inserted. These exhibitions could have been anywhere: Venice, Istanbul, Berlin, São Paulo, or Sharjah (fig. 5).

For instance, the city of Venice is a city on its deathbed, not simply because it is sinking but because it has become a Disneyland, a site of spectacle, a giant tourist park from which daily life is slowly draining away. Its population has halved in the past decade. There was nothing in these two survey exhibitions that questioned the institutional form of the biennial, its particular economic logic within the changing configuration of art practice, or its effects on the urban contexts within which it

Figure 5 Anti-imperialist graffiti from the streets of Venice, June 2005. Photo by author.

arrives every other year. If Venice has turned into a revenue-generating machine, a workplace for the people of Veneto who desert the city in the evening, it is, in part, because it has accepted the role of being a *site*—a beautiful one that leases its gardens and palazzos to this corporate-sponsored art event every other year without having any substantive relationship with the art displayed. In this sense, while Haacke's (in 1993) and Knorr's (in 2005) interventions/subtractions were able to question the material and institutional conditions of the imperial/national mode of appropriation of art, the two group exhibitions failed to engage critically with the new transnational mode of appropriation of art qua *spectacle*.

Acknowledgements

I would like to thank, once again, Jack Amariglio for his editorial help and encouragement. I have liberally borrowed from various conversations with Beral Madra, Teoman Madra, Tulya Madra, Cemal Ener, and Ryvka M. Bar Zohar; this article owes a lot to them. Pelin Tan and the participants in the "Heterotopia" workshop at Istanbul Technical University, the Institute of Social Sciences, the Faculty of Architecture (Summer 2005), helped me work through some of the ideas explored in this essay. Erden Kosova, Kenan Erçel, and Ceren Özselçuk offered their valuable suggestions. The usual disclaimer applies.

References

Adorno, T. 1991. *The culture industry: Selected essays on mass culture.* London: Routledge.

Alberro, A. 1997. The turn of the screw: Daniel Buren, Dan Flavin, and the Sixth Guggenheim International Exhibition. *October* 80: 57–84.

Debord, G. 1995. *The society of the spectacle.* Trans. D. Nicholson-Smith. Cambridge: Zone Books.

Dirlik, A. 2000. Globalization as the end and the beginning of history: The contradictory implications of a new paradigm. *Rethinking Marxism* 12 (4): 4–22.

Fraser, A. 2005. From the critique of institutions to an institution of critique. *Artforum* 44 (1): 278–83.

MacDonald, B. J. 1995. From the spectacle to unitary urbanism: Reassessing Situationist theory. *Rethinking Marxism* 8 (2): 89–111.

Ruccio, D. F., J. Graham, and J. Amariglio. 1997. The good, the bad and the different: Reflections of economic and aesthetic value. In *The value of culture: On the relationship between economics and arts*, ed. A. Klamer, 56–73. Amsterdam: Amsterdam University Press.

RETHINKING MARXISM   VOLUME 18   NUMBER 4   (OCTOBER 2006)

Capital: At Least It Kills Time

(Spinoza, Marx, Lacan, and Temporality)

A. Kiarina Kordela

The theory of temporality and historicity in question is based on two fundamental theses. First, in secular capitalism, semantic (language) and economic systems, and subjectivity—since the speaking subject is the subject of the signifier—are homologous systems of value. Second, time and social reality relate to one another in terms of Spinozist immanent causality, in which the cause (a priori time) is an effect of its own effects (empirical reality). This causality marks not only fantasy and desire but also so-called deductive logic and developmental history. Secular reason (including historiography) must become conscious of its own circularity or fantasmatic character. Addressing leading Marxist approaches to history, such as stage theories of capitalist development and the neo-Spinozist and deconstructionist Left, I argue that our concept of the 'future' must be radically revised. The 'physical' time of decaying bodies is left for a book that will link secular temporality to biopolitics.

Key Words: Cause/Causality, Commodity Fetishism, Fantasy, History, Jouissance, Psychoanalysis, Value

Circulation time cannot be counted as part of value-creating time, for the latter is labour time which objectifies itself in value, and nothing else - ... (... we must distinguish profit from surplus value) ... Circulation time - ... realizes the value created in the production process. It does not increase its quantity, but rather transposes it into another form, from the form of product into that of the commodity, from commodity to that of money etc. ... The necessary tendency of capital is therefore *circulation without circulation time* ... All the requirements of circulation, money, transformation of commodity into money ... etc. ... are all derived from *circulation time*. *Circulation time* is that part of capital which may be regarded as the time it takes to perform its specific motion as capital, as distinct from production time, in which it reproduces itself; and in which it lives ... as capital-in-process, creative capital, sucking its living soul out of labour.

—Marx 1993, *Grundrisse*

Where there is being, infinity is required.

—Lacan, *Book XX. Encore*

ISSN 0893-5696 print/1475-8059 online/06/040539-25
© 2006 Association for Economic and Social Analysis
DOI: 10.1080/08935690600901202

Routledge
Taylor & Francis Group

> So eager are our people to obliterate the present. If from such appearances anyone should draw the conclusion that in reality we have no Emperor, he would not be far from the truth. Over and over again it must be repeated: There is perhaps no people more faithful to the Emperor than ours in the south, but the Emperor derives no advantage from our fidelity ... Peking itself is far stranger to the people in our village than the next world ... We find it more difficult to picture such a city than to believe that Peking and its Emperor are one, a cloud, say, peacefully voyaging beneath the sun in the course of the ages.

—Kafka, "The Great Wall of China"

> The antagonism between the power of landed property, based on personal relations of domination and servitude, and the power of money, which is impersonal, is clearly expressed by the two French proverbs, "Nulle terre sans seigneur [no land without its lord]," and "L'argent n'a pas de maître [money has no master]."

—Marx, *Capital*

Albeit in different ways, antiquity and all the subsequent presecular eras of Hellenistic and medieval theocracy were organized around one and the same persistent opposition: *matter* versus *spirit*. The secular era of capitalist modernity, by contrast, constitutes itself around a radically new opposition: *matter* versus *value*.

The displacement of spirit by the secular function of value entails an unforeseen expansion of the realm of *representation,* insofar as value is an immaterial, abstract symbol that is determined through its differential relation to all other homogeneous symbols. While spirit could manifest itself only in the Word, value has two manifestations: a *semantic* one, as the word or the signifier representing the concept that refers to a thing; and an *economic* one, as the equivalent exchange-value representing the relevant value of a thing (commodity). The advent of secular capitalism amounts to the transformation of economy into a representational system. Consequently, what is usually referred to as *discourse* consists, in secular capitalist modernity, of both semantic representation (language and all culture) and economy, being thus much more inherently linked to power than is generally assumed.

Marx's two seminal works, *Capital* and *Grundrisse,* attempt to articulate (often by means of an allegorical, even mystical poetics rather than by means of an already developed theoretical vocabulary) this quintessential effect of capitalism: the fact that the so-called economic base is itself, contrary to all subsequent widespread and fatal misunderstandings, part of the so-called superstructure. Marx's *Capital* is not only, as Kojin Karatani has argued, "a Kantian 'critique' of economy" (that is, not a phenomenological description of economy but an interrogation as to its transcendental preconditions), but also a veritable *linguistic* theory *avant la lettre* (1995, 91).

What is more, Marx's theory of commodity fetishism, as we shall see, postulates a strict *structural homology* between economic and semantic systems of representation. Here, 'homology' is meant literally, indicating the sharing of the 'same logic'. This common logic entails that if, with Jacques Lacan, the human subject "is the subject of the signifier," then the human subject is also the *subject of value.* Consequently, Marx's *Capital* is also always already a *psychoanalytic* theory, without knowing it (Lacan 1981, 67).

Predicated on the formal homology between economic and semantic systems of representation under the universal aegis of secular value, the present project goes far beyond the fragmented application of certain Lacanian concepts to Marxian theory and, more generally, to society and politics (as in the work of Louis Althusser or Fredric Jameson, to mention only two eminent and influential examples). Here, there is no question of 'application' as both *Marxian and Lacanian theories* are two narratives performing *a transcendental critique of one and the same object: value.* As far as the present argument is concerned, both Marx and Lacan are all four: economical analysts, philosophers, linguists, and psychoanalysts.

Entailed in the position of the present work, which deems Lacanian thought to be the proper postlinguistic sequel to Marxian thought, is the thesis—argued on a sub- or supralevel—that there is an incommensurable discrepancy between Marx's theory and the various theories extant under the rubric of 'Marxism'. To avoid confusion, I use two distinct adjectives: '*Marxian*' for the former, and '*Marxist*' for the latter.

Turning now to the issue of temporality, according to the 'father' of transcendental criticism, Immanuel Kant, "space and time," the pure categories of thought or representation, "together with the appearances in them" are "nothing existing in themselves and outside of my representations" (1977, 82, §52c). Consequently, the representational shift from the domain of spirit to that of value must have also brought about a radical restructuring of space and time, as the preconditions of representation within secular capitalist modernity.

While Gilles Deleuze (1985) has drawn attention to the shift in the conceptualization of space and time effected by the cluster of Kant's three critiques, the present work focuses on time within a broader trajectory that, from Spinoza through Marx to Lacan and us, traverses three centuries of known secular capitalist modernity. The aim is to formulate a properly Spinozist-Marxian-Lacanian theory of temporality and historicity in secular capitalist modernity.

Finally, since representation is always ideological—sustaining a particular body of knowledge, truths, and cultural values, which in turn supports a specific form of power—its transcendental precondition, time, must also bear an intrinsic relation with the sustenance and legitimization of authority, both epistemological (truth) and political (power). Presupposed, therefore, in this theory of temporality and historicity is the interlacing of not simply knowledge, but its transcendental preconditions/categories and politics, including biopolitics. This means that a theory of temporality remains incomplete without a theory of biopolitics. However, the limitations posed by journal publication led me to the decision to include here only that part of the argument referring to time and history, and to reserve the part on biopolitics for a later book that will include the entire argument.

The present article engages itself in dialogue with several contemporary thinkers whose work, more or less directly, plays a role in redefining Marxist thought. In particular, theories of capitalist stage development, the 'neo-Spinozist' Left, and deconstruction are critically, although sometimes appreciatively, represented in this dialogue.

Circulation-Time

My initial hypothesis is that historically available concepts of time are codependent with the ways in which claims to truth, and hence also political authority, are legitimized. If time adjusts itself to the times so that it becomes appropriate for sanctioning historical truths and political power, every time there is a discursive shift in the legitimization of truth and power, there must also exist a shift in the conceptualization of time.

The above hypothesis presupposes that time is paradoxically both a priori and historically determined. Time is simultaneously the transcendent precondition of thought (thought occurs in time and hence presupposes it) *and* yet, it is itself an effect of the very thought it enables. In other words, thought will always already have been determined by the time produced as its effect.

In more general terms, far from being the preceding or transitive cause of the historical in a linear or successive causation, the transcendent is in a differential relation with the historical, being both its cause and effect. The first philosophical articulation of such a causality originates with Spinoza, who argued that "God," the transcendent, "is the immanent, not the transitive, cause of all things" (1985, 428; *Ethics*, pt. 1, prop. 18).

This immanent relation between the historical and the transcendent is also presupposed in Marx's commodity fetishism. There is hardly a Marxist not aware of Hegel's impact on Marx, but few would recognize his debt to Spinozist "pantheism." The latter, of course, is to be understood, as Lacan puts it, not as "what, quite wrongly, has been thought," but "simply [as] the reduction of the field of God to the universality of the signifier" (Lacan 1981, 275).

"Signifier" indicates the secular word, as opposed to the theocratic Word. As long as God was the Creator or transitive cause of the world, He was also the guarantor of, as Foucault has put it, "the similitudes that link the marks to the things designated by them," so that the "Word" consisted of three parts: the mark, the thing, and the similitude because of which the link between "mark" and "thing" was an "organic" bond (1970, 42). That, with Spinoza, "God" is not its transitive cause but "Nature" itself means that "the destruction of the organic" bond has arrived, that the link between mark or "signifier" and the designated thing, the "signified" or concept, is, as Ferdinand de Saussure put it, "arbitrary" (Spinoza 1985, 544; *Ethics*, pt. 4, preface; Foucault 1970, 42; Saussure 1966, 120–1). Henceforth, signifiers and signifieds "are purely differential and negative when considered separately": that is, each is determined within its own synchronic system through its differences from all other elements (signifiers *or* signifieds) of the system, and in itself, without this differentiation, it would be nothing (Saussure 1966, 118–21). In short, the secular signifier is a differential value.

If Marx, unlike his contemporary economists, grasped the mechanism of capital, it was because he applied the pantheistic "universality of the signifier" (value) to the level of economy. He subjected all (commodified) nature to (exchange-)value. Nature—including humans and their labor as "objectified," "congealed," or "abstract human labor"—is not only the vast flock of "objects of utility" (use-value: that is, not abstract value but a concrete, physical thing). It is also the aggregation of "sensuous things which are at the same time suprasensible or social"—that is, "values ... as their [men's] language" (Marx 1990, 150, 165, 167).

Henceforth, the value of a word or a thing or a person is no longer determined by any inherent or inherited qualities of the object in question. It is, rather, as Georg Simmel put it, a "symbol," a "numerical form" or "pure quantity," determined through its relations to and differences from all other symbols (values), "regardless of" its material "specific qualities" (1990, 148, 150). This is why values do not undergo physical decay: a coin retains the value inscribed on it regardless of any possible wearing out of its actual metal, and as for paper money, materially it is practically worthless.

Semantic and economic values exist, therefore, not in a linear time, understood as the continuity past-present-future, but in the *synchronic* temporality in which alone something (value) can be determined differentially. Even though Marx, writing prior to structuralism and linguistics, did not use the present vocabulary, he was fully aware of the fact that circulation-time—the time in which values are exchanged, as opposed to labor- or production-time, in which material objects are produced—designates a synchronic temporality in which 'zero time' or instantaneity and eternity coincide. From the perspective of a conception of time as diachronic succession, capital appears as the paradox of both involving no time and being an eternal "capital-in-process." Thus, instead of using postlinguistic terms such as 'differentiality' or 'synchronicity', Marx employs statements of the type: the "tendency of capital is *circulation without circulation time*" (1993, 671).

What is known as the shift from feudal theocracy to secular capitalist modernity is essentially a shift from the theocracy of the organic link to the pantheism of the arbitrariness of value, whether economic or semantic. This shift is simultaneously one from the theocratic division between the linear, finite time of earthly life and heavenly eternity to the overlap of instantaneity and eternity in the temporality of synchronicity.

And since, in secular modernity, the pantheism of value reigns on both levels, economic and language, the "formal analysis of the commodity," as Alfred Sohn-Rethel succinctly put it, "holds the key not only to the critique of political economy, but also to the historical explanation of the abstract conceptual mode of thinking" (1978, 33). Or, in Slavoj Žižek's paraphrase: "in the structure of the commodity-form it is possible to find ... the network of transcendental categories which constitute the a priori frame of ... knowledge ... the apparatus of categories," in the "Kantian sense" (1989, 16–7).

Marx's commodity fetishism had already superseded the subsequent classical Marxist subordination of the 'superstructure' (language) to the 'base' (economy), advancing instead the thesis that the formal analysis of both the commodity and thought holds the key to the transcendental categories of both—in short, that commodity and thought share the same formal structures insofar as the fields of both consist of values.

Does this mean that linear time—hence all matter, including our bodies, that undergoes physical decay and perishes in it—is an illusion? Does the advent of the historical cluster 'capitalism-secular reason' entail that, all other evidence notwith-standing, in truth we are just one instant and, yet, immortal? What happens to physical bodies and production-time once humans and nature are the subjects no longer of God but of value? This is a crucial question to which we shall return within the context of the temporality of value and, later, biopolitics.

Fantasy

The major epistemological consequence of the pantheism of value and the universalization of differentiality is that, with the advent of secular capitalist modernity, *myths*—whose diachronic narratives had for centuries, from biblical time through all antiquity and theocracy, remained the unchallenged purveyors of truth—lose their legitimacy as such and constitute the realm of sheer fiction. The legitimate source of truth becomes now *logos*—that is, logical deduction, which is a differential and synchronic mode of thought, operating in the mode of immanent causality. If *A* necessarily entails *B*, then *B* also necessarily entails *A* as its presupposition. As Kenneth Burke puts it, "though there is a sense"—a chronological sense—"in which a Father precedes a Son, there is also a sense"—the logical sense—"in which the two states are 'simultaneous,'" since "parents can be parents only insofar as they have offspring, and in this sense the offspring 'makes' the parent" (1970, 32). The realm of logical presuppositions, unlike that of mythical or historical genealogy, is synchronic.

The notorious secular 'historical consciousness' is a systematic and massive reaction to precisely this secular epistemological phenomenon. It is no accident, as Žižek writes in his recapitulation of the philosophical conflict between Hegel and Schelling, that "the central question becomes whether 'the Absolute'" can be presented "through *logos* or *mythos*, through logical deduction or through narra-tion," through the synchronic formalism of "a timeless logical articulation" or through the diachrony of a "temporal appearance of the inner" as "history" (1991, 211). The problem of logical formalism, however, seems to be that it can articulate "the 'synchronic' functioning of the capitalist system," but not "the conditions of its emergence," its cause, which can be described only by taking recourse to a narration (210). As a result, secular discourses devoted their efforts to preventing historio-graphy from slipping out of truth's epistemologically legitimate field into that of fiction—whence the ardent promotion of 'historical consciousness'.

Things seemed to work more or less, except for those occasions when someone would reveal the simultaneity of cause and effect under the façade of diachronic deduction, as Marx did by debunking a notorious 'historical genealogy': the "so-called primitive accumulation." Marx made obvious that the myth or historical narrative meant to explain the generation of capitalism was, in Žižek's words, pure "fantasy": "Long, long ago there [was a] diligent, intelligent, and above all frugal" agent "who "'act[ed] like a capitalist'" prior to the existence of capitalism, and "who did not immediately consume his surplus but wisely reinvested it in production and thus gradually became a capitalist" (Žižek 1991, 210–1; citing Marx 1990, 873). This, in Marx's words, "original sin" of capitalism, far from being a historical truth, is, in

Žižek's words, an "*ideological* myth," a "fantasy," which "has, by definition, the structure of a *story* to be narrated" and is "produced by capitalism retroactively to explain its own genesis and, at the same time, to justify present exploitation: the myth of the 'diligent saving worker'" (Marx 1990, 873; Žižek 1991, 211). So-called historical causality is in truth expressed through the "logic of *fantasy*," which, albeit manifest as a diachronic narrative, is "circular" since it "presupposes what it purports to explain" (Žižek 1991, 211). Far from expressing the truth about the linear genealogy of any given historical state, it only reaffirms (or, alternatively, depending on its content, challenges) the ideology sustaining that state.

It follows that secular thought is incapable of providing diachronic or transitive causes. All secular causality, logical and (presumably) genealogical, is immanent: that is, fantasy. This means, first, that secular thought always arrives there from where it starts (without knowing it)—"the real is that which always returns to the same place"—and, second, if truth emerges only as a synchronic re-finding of itself, then really fantasmatic is the illusion that it emerges in a diachronic succession (Lacan 1981, 49). All causality is structured as fantasy, but *truly fantasmatic (i.e., illusory) is the assumption that history is a diachronic narrative*. To "traverse the fundamental fantasy" means to get out of diachrony, to arrive finally at synchrony (271). Non-fantasy is what cannot be *traversed*.[1]

Crucially, this conclusion does not mean that whatever presents itself as a diachronic narrative should be dismissed as an epistemologically illegitimate mode of thought. Quite the contrary, it means that it should be reduced to its synchronic logic so that the truth underlying the fantasy is revealed. The lesson of Marx's debunking of capitalism's "original sin" is not that history is epistemologically illegitimate, but that it is ideological. To traverse the fantasy means to reveal the truth about the ideological fantasy, the desire that motivates history.

Far from drawing such conclusions, however, secular discourses opted for other paths. Thus, the call for historical consciousness finds, through the challenge posed by the revelation of history as fantasy, its corollary countertendency: the increasingly unanimous fervor to sustain synchronic *logos* as the legitimate source of truth, and to relegate not only explicit myths but also history to the realm of *epistemologically illegitimate* fantasy. Popularized by Nietzsche, the latter tradition is arguably the dominant in postmodernity, if it is not, as is entailed in Fredric Jameson's conception of postmodernism, its very essence (see, for instance, Jameson 1991). In opposition to this 'postmodernism' the various stage theories act as the remaining proponents of 'historical consciousness'. And neither party ceases its 'struggle' for a moment to

---

1. Although never referred to as such, both Benjamin's conception of history, as presented in his seminal article "Theses on the Philosophy of History," and Freud's "Nachträglichkeit" [belatedness] are applications of immanent causality in history, collective and individual, respectively (see Benjamin 1969, 253–64; Freud 1999, 12:54–75). Whether properly or not, this Spinozist conception of history has had, notably since Louis Althusser, a large impact on a line of leftist thinkers, which we shall address below (see, for instance, Althusser 1996, 71–86). While the present work focuses on Spinoza's centrality for a secular conceptualization of time and historicity, I address the intrinsic relation between Spinozist and psychoanalytic, notably Lacanian, thought elsewhere (see Kordela 2007).

raise the question: if all secular causality is immanent, then why should either formalism or historicism be closer to truth than the other?

The debate is fake because there is *no* epistemological distinction between *logos* and *mythos*. Both are synchronic, operating in the mode of immanent causality. This is apparent also in the contradiction in Žižek's afore-cited passage: *logos* is described as *both* "logical deduction," which as such is supposed to be transitive (*A* entails *B*, *B* entails *C*, and so on), *and* "a timeless logical articulation," which, being logical, is reciprocal (if *A* entails *B*, *B* presupposes *A*), and as such does not unfold in (linear) time but is rather precisely "timeless." Both *logos* and *mythos* are structured according to the logic of fantasy, but what is *illusory* is the assumption that they operate according to transitive causality—that they are a transitive deduction, whether it is called logical or historical.

Things are exactly the other way around: prior to the advent of psychoanalysis, all secular reason, while all the while calling itself *logos,* had understood itself as *mythos*—that is, as diachronic thought operating in the mode of transitive causality. This is what philosophy traditionally has understood under "logical deduction," which is why 'circular' (immanent) thought has always been dismissed as illegitimate or false.

God Is Unconscious

The contempt for circular thought is already evident in the philosophical response to what we could call the original sin of secular reason: Descartes' "radical doubt." It introduces the paranoiac anxiety that a *genius malignus* (a malign spirit) might deceive us into believing that all material bodies surrounding us, including our own, exist, when in truth they may be a sheer illusion (see Descartes 1968, 102–2).[2] Given what precedes this point in Descartes' argument, the inference that would *appear* to be closer to a transitive deduction is, as a matter of fact, that, as long as "I think," matter is a mere illusion, and "therefore, I am not"—or, as Valéry put it, *"tantôt je pense, tantôt je suis"* [at times I think, and at times I am], and, to put it in our terms, "as long as I am a value, I am not a physical body" (as cited in Arendt 1978, I, 201). Descartes, however, opted, as is known, to derive existence from thought. But he could do so only by returning, through the back door, truth to the hands of God. If I am deceivable and hence imperfect, in order not to be deceived there must be some other perfect being that shows me truth and not illusion; therefore, God must exist, for only God "cannot be a deceiver," for "He" alone is perfect and "the natural light teaches us that deceit stems from some defect" (Descartes 1968, 131). Time and again, philosophers have declared Descartes' reasoning to be false or epistemologically illegitimate due to its circular logic—the fact that it presupposes what it

---

2. Lacan refers to "the social dialectic that structures human knowledge as paranoiac" (1977, 3). 'Paranoia,' of course, indicates here not a clinically pathological state of subjectivity but a structure marking 'normal' subjectivity, such as when one is not sure whether one's interlocutor is telling the truth or attempting to deceive.

purports to prove: 'there is truth; therefore, beyond my imperfection, there must be perfection; therefore there is truth.'

The issue at stake once truth is handed back to "the perfect God" is, as Lacan put it, that God's "truth is the nub of the matter, since, whatever he might have meant, would always be *the* truth—even if he had said that two and two make five, it would have been true" (1981, 36). Indeed, "two and two make five" is no more arbitrary a statement than "I think, therefore, I am," which nevertheless dominated the Western imaginary for centuries. The "extraordinary consequences that have stemmed from this handing back of truth into the hands of the other, in this instance, the perfect God," can be understood only in relation to the fact that philosophy declared Descartes' circular syllogism, hence God as the guarantor of truth, illegitimate (Lacan 1981, 36).

If circular syllogisms are illegitimate, then all secular reason is illegitimate. If Descartes claims that "I think, therefore, I am," whereas I could argue that "I think, therefore, I am not," it is because he presupposes a benevolent God, as derived from the Christian tradition, whereas I presuppose the Marxian opposition between exchange- and use-value. *Logos* could prove either that existence derives from thought or that it does not, but it can prove any *one* of the two statements as true only on the ground of a presupposition that will always already have been posed by its eventual conclusion (that existence either does or does not derive from thought). "If God is benevolent, I am" is the same as the statement "If I am, God is benevolent," just as "If God is value, I am not" is the same as the statement "If I am not, God is value"—that the hypothesis presupposes the apodosis means precisely that it cannot be decided which of the two comes first in linear time. The apodosis is itself the hypothesis.

Immanuel Kant had the spirit—and that in the heart of the Enlightenment—to show that pure reason, understood as *transitive* deduction, is inherently self-contra-dictory, producing antinomic pairs of mutually exclusive truths or untruths (see Kant 1998, particularly 411–550; A 341/B 399–A 567/B 595). As far as transitive deduction is concerned, both "I think, therefore, I am" and "I think, therefore, I am not" are true (or untrue). To prove the one as true and the other as false, therefore, something beyond transitive deduction must be added to it, because of which the deduction is in appearance transitive but in truth circular. This is why once he finished with "pure reason," Kant felt compelled to turn to something he called "practical reason." But this distinction cannot take us far.

Neither can the distinction between *logos* qua synchronic formalism and *mythos* qua diachronic narration or deduction, since the said distinction is not one between two really different modes of reasoning but one between two self-perceptions of *logos* itself. The one is conscious of its circular structure, and the entailed fact that its certainty derives from a presupposed God that it produces as its own surplus—insofar as 'God' indicates the function of providing certainty or the guarantee of truth. The other perceives itself precisely as *mythos*—that is, as a transitive deduction, ignoring both its own circularity and its surplus God.

The difference between theocratic and secular reason lies not in the presence or absence of the function of 'God' as the guarantor of certainty, but in that in the former God is posited indeed transitively, as the prior to thought, while in the latter *God is posited retroactively as the surplus of thought itself*.

Due to this difference, theocracy was monotheistic, whereas secular modernity is pantheistic: anything can theoretically function as God. Like capital, which is "money which is worth more money, value which," due to surplus-value, "is greater than itself," *logos*, too, is something greater than itself due to its own surplus, God, as the guarantor of its truths (Marx 1990, 257). In secular capitalist modernity, *mythos* is a secondary phenomenon, a defense mechanism, through which *logos* remains unconscious of its God as its own surplus. This is why, as Lacan has argued, the "true formula of atheism," that is, of properly secular thought, is not "God is dead" but *"God is unconscious"* (1981, 59). Lacan's insistence that the subject of psychoanalysis is the Cartesian subject is strictly correlative to this assertion.

The present argument sheds some light on the psychoanalytic distinction between fantasy as the *real* kernel of reason—its unconscious—and fantasy as ideological fantasy and illusion. God is unconscious; by contrast, the self-perception of *logos* as godless transitive deduction or *mythos* is ideological fantasy. The former is structurally necessary (without *some* God, secular reason is stuck in its Kantian antinomy); the latter is not.

The issue at stake cannot be settled by simply reducing, in deconstructive fashion, *logos* and *mythos* to one another's supplements. Foucault opted in this regard for the deconstructive path and established a supplementary relation between *logos* as synchronic formalism and *mythos* as diachronic, hence teleological narrative, whether in the form of "eschatology" (history) or "exegesis" (interpretation). In Foucault's words, "in order to formalize . . . is it not necessary to have practiced some minimum of exegesis, and at least interpreted all those mute forms as having the intention of meaning something?" (1970, 299). Appearances to the contrary, the logic of sheer supplementarity always ends up, as Foucault's book itself evidences, with the radicalization of formalism into an eternal recurrence of the Same, which is subsequently recognized as the sole truth, and the dismissal of "eschatology"—Marx being reduced to one of its eminent examples—as illegitimate, by which are meant all three: "essentialist," "metaphysical," and "wish-fulfilling" (320).

Rather, the point is that *logos is by structural necessity wish-fulfilling, metaphysical, and essentialist* insofar as these terms indicate nothing more than the necessary presupposition of a surplus to transitive deduction that comes to perform the same function God used to perform in theocracy—namely, to provide certainty as the ground of truth. The psychoanalytic reference to the unconscious is a reminder that if the transcendent surplus of *logos* is dismissed as illegitimate in secular epistemology, it does not magically disappear; rather, its presupposition remains necessary for the sustenance of secular truths, while its fetishistic disavowal becomes equally necessary, as the history of secular philosophy and politics attests.

Stages of Development and Eternal Laws

The problem of the various Marxist eschatologies is not their wish but the fact that, however many years of history they might traverse, they never traverse the fantasy that they *are* historical narratives.[3] And this even if, as is usually the case, the fantasy and its underlying wish are openly, if not programmatically, stated.

The obligatory agenda of any 'leftist' "stage theories of capitalist development," as Bruce Norton indicates in his critique of Fredric Jameson's "totalizing theory," consists in treating capitalism, not simply as a "totality" but as a "totality on a mission" (1995, 62–3). Norton sees in the "presuppositions at the core of any Marxian economic analysis" the historical necessity that the totality of capitalism marches toward "its *telos* of progressively dysfunctional and irrational capitalist functioning" (61, 63). Although, "like other Marxian stages theories of capitalist development," Jameson's own stage theory also "links concepts of the basic 'nature' of 'capital' to certain necessities," its faux pas consists in presenting the postmodern stage of capitalism, Norton continues, as "a moment of capital 'purer' and more encompassing than ever," in which "there are no barriers signaling capitalism's approaching end ... but the opposite, marks of the system's all-pervasive, subject-redefining power" (61, 66). Regardless of whether Norton adequately represents Jameson's work, what he actually does is to reconfirm, against his intentions, the point made here. Far from constituting any deductive historical narrative, stage theories are organized around a desire for a specific end. From the perspective of stage theories, Jameson's work is read the same way one could read Orwell's *1984,* even if the latter does not offer a whole stage theory but only the 'last stage'—for what matters in stage theories is not the deduction of stages but the *finale.* The logic of stage theories does not differ from the old Hollywood motto: "if the end is good, all is good."

It is perhaps time for the Left to pay more attention to ideological mechanisms whose propaganda has historically proved more effective than its own. There is something to be learned from the fact that a happy ending is no longer a sine qua non in Hollywood. Norton's argument presupposes not only that Marxian premises necessarily lead to capitalism's dysfunction—a presupposition that itself presupposes the arbitrary (i.e., fantasmatic) decision to opt for 'contingent' as opposed to 'necessity' theories regarding the function of crises in capitalism—but also a quasi-Pavlovian stimulus/response mechanism, according to which people are supposed to take whatever is presented to them in culture as the 'good' example to reenact in reality. What if 'revolutionary consciousness' is today more effectively constituted through 'bad' examples, such as the presentation of late capitalism as an Orwellian fantasy? Why am I supposed to develop the desire to undermine capitalism by reading the *Communist Manifesto* and not *1984*?

Furthermore, one must also raise the most fundamental question as to what really is 'revolutionary'. Is a 'revolution' that eventually reveals itself as having always already been one more crisis within capitalism, necessary for its own reinforcement, indeed a 'revolution'? Almost a century after the 'glorious October revolution' and

3. As the Japanese philosopher and literary critic, Kojin Karatani (who, unlike Foucault, reads Marx as a formalist comparable to Kant rather than eschatologist) argues, "speaking of the future was" for Marx "itself reactionary" (2003, ix). Indeed, "in his entire corpus Marx only rarely dealt with a program for the future: in *The Manifesto of the Communist Party,* which was a collaboration with Engels, and in *Critique of the Gotha Programme,* which was written simply as a critical commentary on someone else's program" (Karatani 1995, 187).

decades after the collapse of the former East bloc and subsequent total globalization of capitalism, it is high time we began posing this question.

Since what appears to be a teleological diachrony in history is in truth an ideological, circular, self-reflective, and self-justifying syllogistic loop that presupposes its own end, a *nonillusory* conception of history must be structured in a *properly* fantasmatic way that has traversed the fantasy that 'historical periods' decline because their logical contradictions increasingly produce, in time, by some presumed historical necessity, the empirical conditions or stages required for their demise and succession by another period.

The Spinozist-Marxian-Lacanian line of thought constitutes a radical alternative to the centuries-old tradition of historicism, indicating that in secular capitalist modernity, history can be properly conceived only as a synchronic system whose elements are not periods but *synchronic blocks*. Each block is defined by its own *formal logic,* whose structure can be described only in terms of the formal logic of the *present block*. Past, present, and future—all occur now. Each *historical block* may consist of *any* number of *stages,* each exhibiting any number of contingent differences from the others, but all of them constitute stages of one and the same block because, whatever their *concrete contingent shapes,* they are *all manifestations of one and the same formal structure*. If there is any teleology in the stages, this is their *telos* to *embody in reality the formal structure* of the existing block *now*.

It follows that the criterion of what constitutes a proper revolution is neither the amount of shed blood caused by it nor its appearance as an event realizing some presumed historical necessity, but its knowledge regarding the *formal* conditions that need to be changed, so that its effect is not yet another stage—disguised as crisis—within the present block, but a really other historical block. To obtain this knowledge, one must examine not the genealogical succession of stages in capitalism but "the eternal laws of commodity-exchange" that define *all* stages of capitalism, regardless of all other contingent differences among them (Marx 1990, 301). The end of capitalism is not to be found in its mutable and contingent stages but in its *eternal laws*—which, incidentally, is also what Marx was after.[4]

Old and New Masters,
Old and New Historical Blocks

The central formal eternal law of commodity exchange is that, whatever contingency it may involve, it always procures surplus-value. Capitalism's past, from the slave

---

4. As Eugene Holland argues, drawing on Pierre Macherey's conclusive opposition between Spinoza and Hegel, "a Spinozian-Marxist politics would reject all forms of teleologism" (§27). This does not mean that history would be "bereft of any shape or direction whatsoever," but that it is governed by these "'laws'... diagnosed by Marx," which reveal the *"contradictory"* character of "capitalism as a mode of production." These "contradictions" expressed in Marx's "eternal laws" "constitute," therefore, "the *motor of history*," but not in the sense of *"dialectical* contradictions in the teleological sense understood by Hegelian Marxism, i.e. as destined for synthesis/resolution at some shining moment in the future" (§28). (See also Macherey).

systems of pagan antiquity to theocratic feudalism, can be conceived only as the negative of this eternal law defining our present historical block: if capitalism involves surplus-value and is thus a system of disequilibrium, then its past must have been an economic system of equilibrium, with no surplus. Concomitantly, due to the structural homology between economic and semantic systems, the absence of surplus-value must also be reflected on the semantic level, which will also be described in negative terms, as one of equilibrium, with no unconscious surplus required to ground truth and political authority.

Thus, the formal structure of the discourse (something which, we recall, is both economic and semantic) of any presecular/precapitalist block can be represented as in Lacan's succinct formula of the discourse of the Master:

$$\frac{S1}{\$} \rightarrow \frac{S2}{a}$$

Here, knowledge (*savoir*) and vassals are effectively indistinguishable (both symbolized with S2), since the unambiguous raison-d'être of both is to serve the master (S1). The master's address ($\rightarrow$) to the slave is tantamount to the command that the latter put all the knowledge he might posses and all his labor to the service of the former. And by working, the slave produces ever more products and knowledge (*a*), but crucially, the latter play no role in the slave's knowledge of what the master wants, his truth. For above and beyond any practical knowledge and the "beaucoup de choses" [many things] he "sait" [knows], the slave knows with absolute and a priori certainty "ce que le maître veut" [what the master wants]—namely, that the slave work for him. This is so "même si celui-ci ne le sait pas" [even if he (the master) does not know it himself, even if he himself is inconsistent (\$), "ce qui est le cas ordinaire, car sans cela" [which is the usual case, for otherwise], as Hegel has made amply clear, "il ne serait pas un maître" [he would not be a master] (Lacan 1991, 34). What is hidden (placed in the lower left position in the formula) is the master's own inconsistency (\$), for the slave knows nothing about it.

The "essence du maître" [essence of the master] remains throughout all history the fact "qu'il ne sait pas ce qu'il veut" [that he does not know what he wants], but the crucial thing is *whether the slave is convinced that he knows what the master wants* (34). The array of new phenomena specific to the way in which political power is exercised within the era of capitalism and secular reason (e.g., ideology, hegemony, noncoercive coercion, and biopolitics) entails that in all history prior to capitalist modernity, the slave did not need to draw on his knowledge in order to know what the master wanted. The truth of the precapitalist master, so far as the slave is concerned, preceded the latter's knowledge (*savoir*), which was itself a derivative by-product of this truth.

The difference between the classical or "maître antique" [old master] and the "maître moderne, que l'on appelle capitaliste, est une modification dans la place du savoir" [modern master, whom we call capitalist, is a modification in the place of knowledge] (Lacan 1991, 34). With capitalist secular modernity, the position of mastery, which is always "celle de gauche" [that on the left] in the graph of a discourse, comes to be occupied by knowledge itself and thus to form what Lacan calls the University discourse (5):

$$\frac{S2}{S1} \rightarrow \frac{a}{\$}$$

Now master and knowledge are effectively indistinguishable (S2), for knowledge is "non pas savoir-de-tout ... mais tout-savoir" [not knowledge of everything ... but all-knowledge]: that is, "rien d'autre que savoir" [nothing other than knowledge]—not mastery or power, but pure knowledge, which, as such, is said to be "objective knowledge" (34). As a consequence, what is hidden in the University discourse is no longer (\$), the fact that the master himself does not know what he wants, but the fact that knowledge (S2) *is* mastery and power (S1). How is this practically possible? Because knowledge is now secular, that is, both "objective"—presenting itself as (if it were) operating on purely transitive deduction—*and* lacking (a ground), so that it requires a surplus—fantasy (*a*)—in order to sustain itself as (presumably) "objective." Thus, the entrance of the secular subject-slave to discourse, the body of knowledge, entails his split (\$), since he speaks through something that presents itself as "objective" knowledge while, in truth, it relies on fantasy. It is only insofar as the slave's fantasy adjoins the truth of the master that the latter comes to appear as (if it were) "objective knowledge."

The difference between the "old" and the "new" slaves is the same as that between "landed property" and "money": "no land" and no 'old slave' "without its" or his "lord," while "money" and the 'modern slave' have "no master." Unlike the discourse of the Master, the "hidden" in the University discourse fulfills a function necessary for the slave to sustain the truth of the master: the 'truth' that there is no master, or, what amounts to the same, the 'truth' that knowledge is 'objective'. This is why, once in the historical block represented by the University discourse, the "hidden" must be taken into account as an epistemological and political function—the function of the unconscious, which is one pertaining specifically to secular capitalist modernity and its Cartesian subject-slave.

The brief description of the university discourse therefore is: knowledge (S2) addresses the unconscious fantasy (a) of the subject, which, at the cost of splitting itself (\$), provides the required surplus so that the said knowledge appears as "objective" and not as a body of knowledge serving a certain power (S1).

Consequently, ever since the advent of secular capitalist modernity, "savoir" [knowledge], as something which "puisse faire totalité" [is capable of making a totality], is "immanente au politique en tant que tel" [immanent to politics as such], for knowledge, the new locus of power, can make a (consistent) totality only if the subject provides it with a surplus (Lacan 1991, 4). The moment knowledge requires an unconscious surplus in order to obtain the appearance of consistent objective knowledge, ideological fantasy emerges as an indispensable political factor. Ideology, in turn, is predicated on a fetishistic split between (unconscious) knowledge and (fantasmatic) belief: 'although I know that my acts and thoughts are dictated by the master/power, I believe that they are dictated by objective knowledge.'[5] (It is knowledge, not belief, that is unconscious.)[6] The notorious Hegelian dialectic of master and slave refers to the times of value in which, the more the modern slave knows that he is a slave, the more he believes that he is his own sole master. Thus, we arrive at the possibility of the widely praised fantasy of the 'freedom of the individual'.[7] On the pillar of this belief rests the mechanism of internalized authority and noncoercive coercion.

Franz Kafka seems to have grasped the strict correlation between the fantasy of 'freedom' and the fantasy that history takes place in diachronic time. By falling prey to "appearances," such as history unfolding "in the course of the ages," we also "believe that Peking and the Emperor are one, a cloud, peacefully voyaging beneath the sun" in this temporal course. Thus, no sooner do we "obliterate the present" in which we really live than it becomes "more difficult to picture such a city." Consequently, should anyone "draw the conclusion that in reality we have no Emperor, he would not be far from the truth," even as, of course, it must "over and over again ... be repeated" that "there is perhaps no people more faithful to the Emperor than ours."

The constitution of the modern master-slave entails various paradoxical cultural and political phenomena, contemporary American politics being a shining example. The bewilderment often expressed by the 'democrats' in the face of the results of the recent presidential elections in the United States only perpetuates an ideological, reactionary fantasy—the belief, against all conspicuous evidence to the contrary, that knowledge is a consistently objective system.[8] Alas, this does not mean that the critics

5. This is the logic of fetishism as defined by Freud: that is, as the logic through which the subject disavows something it knows to be true ("I may know very well that X is true, but nevertheless I act as if I did not know"). Freud's conception of fetishism goes one step beyond Marx's commodity fetishism ("they do this without being aware") by taking into account the cynicism that keeps 'doing this' even while 'being aware of' the truth about it (Marx 1990, 166–7). (For Freud's concept of fetishism, see Freud 1999, 14:311–7.) Freud's fetishism relates to the as-if principle, as derived from Jeremy Bentham's "Philosophy of the 'As If'" (1932) and as revised by the neo-Kantian philosopher Hans Vaihinger (1924). Octave Mannoni (1969) further developed the as-if principle as the logic of *"je sais bien, mais quand meme"* [I know well, but nevertheless]. The as-if logic has had a large impact on the works of, among others, Lacan (1981, 163; 1992, 12, 187, 228), Althusser (1971, especially 127–86), and Žižek (1991, 1996).
6. In his analysis of Hitchcock's *Psycho*, Žižek writes: "'I know very well that event X will take place (that Arbogast will be murdered), yet I do not fully believe it (so I'm none the less surprised when the murder actually takes place." Desire therefore, Žižek argues, resides not "in the belief" but "in the knowledge." From this, he infers: "The horrifying reality that one refuses to 'believe in,' to accept, to integrate into one's symbolic universe, is none other than the Real of one's desire, and the unconscious belief (that X could not actually happen) is ultimately a defense against the Real of desire" (1992, 231). It remains unclear to me whether we concur at this point as it seems to me that, on the one hand, Žižek argues that the "Real of desire," that which one refuses "to integrate into one's symbolic universe," and hence the unconscious, resides in knowledge, but, on the other hand, he designates the "belief" also as "unconscious" (231).
7. Lacan elaborates on the function of this fantasy particularly in his third seminar (1993).
8. Joan Copjec (1994) explains the election of presidents in the United States, such as Ronald Reagan, through precisely this logic.

of this politics necessarily transcend these paradoxes. To recall the paradox of stage theories, a body of knowledge can openly declare as its a priori presupposition the end of history as the end of capitalism *and* nevertheless reproduce narratives that present this a priori presupposition as the outcome of a transitive deduction. In every ideological system, ideological fantasy is precisely a belief determined to remain blind to the publicly displayed (i.e., known) split inhering in its 'objective knowledge'.

What generates and sustains this belief? Lacan calls the cause or ground of belief "surplus-enjoyment" (*plus-de-jouir*), which is nothing more than the mere fact that 'objective knowledge' *is* split. The fantasmatic belief is caused by the mere conspicuousness of the fact that 'objective knowledge' does not work. If one asks about a "cause" only when "something … doesn't work," it is because the cause of the question and, hence, the answer, is itself the very fact that something does not work (Lacan 1981, 22). If the subject derives a surplus-enjoyment from the Other's inconsistency—the fact that 'objective knowledge' does not work—it is precisely because the subject's loyalty to the Other cannot be 'objectively' justified. Rather, it can be explained only as a kind of (Kierkegaardian) unconditional devotion or sacrifice, comparable to the sense experienced by the religious believer. This sense is *jouis-sens* [enjoyment of sense]—that is, an enjoyment relying on the sliding of 'sense' from the semantic to the sensual level; when 'objective knowledge' does not make sense, one can always enjoy the sublime sense of one's unshakable, absolute devotion to it. And just like in many religions, including Christianity, all human enjoyment is eventually subjugated to the highest enjoyment of devotedly serving God, all secular enjoyment (*jouissance*) is eventually subjugated to that of devotedly serving the Other (*jouis-sens*), remaining faithful to it against all evidence of its inconsistency.

The fact that this unconditional devotion amounts to the sacrifice of any form of enjoyment (*jouissance*) other than *joui-sens,* the enjoyment of the sense of this devotion itself, is not conveyed in the English translation. Unlike 'surplus-enjoy-ment', the French *plus-de-jouir* means both 'more enjoyment' and 'no more enjoyment'. Only the Other itself continues to derive enjoyment (*jouissance*) insofar as it enjoys its sustenance in the position of the master, no matter what it says. Even if it says that two and two make five, the Other invariably emerges as omnipresent and omniscient, since the subject's *jouis-sens* allows everything to count as 'pure' or 'objective knowledge'.

This is where the analogy between *jouis-sens* and religious belief ceases. Like the old slave, the religious believer knows prior to any other knowledge what his master, God, wants from him: to serve Him. The modern Other is sustained on the absence of an identifiable Will. A popular approach to Spinoza naively assumes that the liberation of people from all forms of oppression lies in understanding that God has no Will. Historical reality, however, shows that the same understanding paradoxically leads to the impression that if there is no Will, then, there is no God or Master, either.

Here is also where the analogy between the present model and the Nietzschean explanation of noncoercive coercion by means of the 'will to power' breaks. What Nietzsche ignored is that the public display of the Other's inconsistency only reinforces the subject's *jouis-sens,* hence the subject's subjugation to the Other's power. Nietzsche's analysis could not have a subversive effect either in a presecular discourse (where it would be redundant since it only reveals what the slave already knows as the a priori truth of the master) or in the secular. Just as deconstruction only reinforces devoted belief in metaphysical functions, the true believer of stage theories is not going to be converted just by being exposed to the inconsistency of stage theories. Conversion is not a matter of sheer enlightenment, for it presupposes an intervention on the level of *jouis-sens*—that is, the *link between the failure of semantic sense and sensation*. Otherwise it makes no sense to speak of biopolitics.

But to remain for now on the difference between the two types of masters, just as in the precapitalist past economy did not involve surplus-value (*plus-value*), the presecular authority of the Master did not rely on a surplus-enjoyment (*plus-de-jouir*). This is not to say that the ancient and the theocratic discourses were consistent, but that their inconsistency did not in any way affect the a priori, explicit truth of the Master. The multiplicity of conflicting ancient myths and the endless theological debates could take place only without impunity, under the strict supervision of an authority whose right of intervention remained a priori unchallengeable by any possible criticism. Once this a priori truth is hidden, we find ourselves in the historical block of secular power that takes upon itself the 'duty' to protect the 'right of free expression'. Its authority relies on 'objective truths' whose inconsistency must be revealed publicly, so that the subjects themselves are led to sustain them through their devoted enjoyment of sense.

In conclusion, the question concerning a properly Marxian historical analysis is not 'what caused this shift' in which the surplus, economic and semantic, begins to adjoin itself, on the one hand, to money, which thus becomes capital, and, on the other hand, to the truth of the Master, which thereby becomes secular. The shift in itself is an a priori fact. As Lacan put it in his seventeenth seminar:

> Something changed in the discourse of the master at a certain moment in history. We are not going to break our heads to figure out whether it was because of Luther or Calvin, or I do not know what circulation of ships around Genoa or in the Mediterranean sea, or elsewhere, since the important point is that from a certain day on the surplus-enjoyment [*plus-de-jouir*] starts to be counted, accounted, totalized. Here starts what one calls accumulation of capital. (1991, 207; translation mine)

Rather, the proper question is concerned with grasping *wherein* the said shift consists: *what is the formal structure of the shift?* Lacan's response to this properly Marxian question is: "the impotence of adjoining the surplus-enjoyment to the truth of the master ... the impotence of this junction is suddenly voided. The surplus-value adjoins itself to capital—no problem, they are homogenous, we are within values" (207; translation mine).[9]

---

9. "Quelque chose a changé dans le discourse du maître à partir d'un certain moment de l'histoire. Nous n'allons pas nous casser les pieds à savoir si c'est à cause de Luther, ou de Calvin, ou de je ne sais quel trafic de navires autour de Gênes, ou dans la mer Méditerranée, ou ailleurs, car le point important est qu'à partir d'un certain jour, le plus-de-jouir se compte, se comptabilise, se totalise. Là commence ce que l'on appelle accumulation du capital ... l'impuissance à faire le joint du plus-de-jouir à la vérité du maître ... l'impuissance de cette jonction est tout d'un coup vidée. La plus-value s'adjoint au capital—pas de problème, c'est homogène, nous sommes dans les valeurs."

And once we are within values, we are also within their mode of temporality, circulation-time, in which genealogy is an illusion. The question about the possibility of a historical block other than both the 'present' and the 'past' cannot, therefore, be posed in terms of 'what would cause' the emergence of this other block. Rather, the question is what the formal structure of such a block could be. A response can be derived only negatively from the structures of the 'past' and 'present' blocks. A 'future'-other block of secular capitalism would presuppose (*a*) that there is a surplus (unlike in the 'past') and (*b*) that the surplus does not adjoin itself to capital and 'objective knowledge' (unlike in the 'present'). The fantasmatic surplus is itself necessary, for there can be no secular knowledge without it. But it must present itself as what it is, fantasy, resisting its assimilation by knowledge *cum* transitive deduction.

By contrast, when one argues that historical stages, whatever they may be, constitute a transitive succession that necessarily (i.e., according to the laws of objective knowledge) leads either to the eternal perpetuation of capitalism (as in the liberalist progressivist myths, including those of postmodern capitalism as the end of history) or to its inevitable collapse (as in the traditional Marxist stage theories), one forces surplus-enjoyment to adjoin itself to 'objective knowledge'. Far from being necessary or inevitable, the emergence of a historical block really other than the one existing under the auspices of capital and 'objective knowledge' is contingent upon desire. As for its ontological status, the other block is not something to be realized in some 'future'. Like the "unconscious," the 'other' block "is neither being, nor non-being, but the unrealized . . . in that non-temporal locus" of "einer anderen Lokalität . . . another space, another scene" alongside the *"here and now"* (Lacan 1981, 30, 56).

Outside Credit-Time:
A Desiring Crystal-Image

Let us now turn to those contemporary leftist theories that, unlike stage theories which are predicated on Hegelian dialectical teleologism, tend to conceive of the temporality of secular capitalism more or less in terms of circulation-time. These are basically two: the so-called neo-Spinozist, and the deconstructionist.

As we saw, stage theories reduce the surplus of desire to the necessity of some presumably transitively deduced law. By contrast, the neo-Spinozists either collapse the object of desire and circulation-time or construct desire as the necessary end point of some diachronic trajectory (e.g., lines of flight) that is itself necessarily produced by circulation-time. We could call the first variant of neo-Spinozism the model of absolute immanence insofar as the future *is* (always already) the present, or, in my terms, the other block *is* (always already) *this* block. The second variant would then be the model of relative immanence insofar as the future or other block is external to the present or this block, albeit necessarily entailed by the latter. Antonio Negri with Michael Hardt and Gilles Deleuze with Félix Guattari can be taken as the most prominent proponents of absolute and relative immanence, respectively. The deconstructionist Left can be seen as a hybrid form of 'Spinozism' and 'Hegelianism' in which time is conceived as circulation-time—that is, in terms of Spinozist immanent causality but with no otherness ('future') whatsoever, both because the same *is* the other and because immanent causality is supplemented by a transitive or teleological causality in a diachrony whose end, unlike in the traditional under-standing of Hegel, is eternally deferred.

Turning first to relative immanence, in his by now classic two volumes on cinema, Deleuze advances nothing less than a theory of historical time within secular modernity. The advent of post–World War II cinema, Deleuze argues, constitutes a shift from linear or diachronic "action-time," which characterized prewar classical cinema, to a synchronic time in which the historical relation between past and present becomes a logico-causal relation between the manifest present and its transcendental preconditions (past). If with Deleuze, we call the entirety of time the "crystal-image," its manifest present aspect the "actual image," and its presup-posed past aspect the "virtual image," then the relation between present and past reveals itself as follows: "The present is the actual image, and its contemporaneous past is the virtual image, the image in a mirror" (Deleuze 1995, 79). In the crystal-image, "each side," the actual and the virtual, takes "the other's role in a relation which we must describe as reciprocal presupposition, or reversibility," whereby the past is the precondition of the present and vice versa (69). Thus, although past and present are "distinct," they are "indiscernible," so that "the actual and the virtual ... are in continual exchange" (70).

Let us pause here to note that, as the present argument indicates, even though cinema, as Deleuze's analysis shows, may indeed have been capable of explicitly representing immanent causality as the law governing secular temporality only since the end of World War II, this mode of temporality marks secular capitalist modernity since its inception, as is indicated through both Spinoza's seventeenth-century conceptualization of it and capitalism's self-presentation as caused by the "original sin" of "primitive accumulation." The possibility of postwar cinema should rather be seen as only one of the phenomena accompanying the overarching challenges increasingly posed since the late nineteenth century to the tradition of 'historical consciousness'.[10]

To continue with Deleuze's scheme, what remains resolutely outside the crystal-image is the future. This lies at the end of a linear temporality marked by transitive causality. There has never been a future in cinema, Deleuze argues, since cinema,

---

10. Similar to Deleuze's analysis of cinema after World War II, Walter Benjamin's (1977) analysis of seventeenth-century German Baroque drama (*Trauerspiel*) offers a remarkable account of the secular binary sign (allegory), as it functions in all secular modernity (including postmodernity), while presupposing that prior to it the sign (symbol) was ternary, in the exact Foucauldian sense. The various cultural articulations, ranging from Baroque allegory and Spinoza's conception of God as the immanent cause of nature to postwar cinema, are different historical representations of the formal structure of the temporality of secular modernity. No "eternal law" is to be derived from the contingent fact that secular temporality finds its more pronounced representations in the cultural productions of particularly the early and late stages of capitalism: the seventeenth and twentieth centuries, respectively. This phenomenon is due to the equally contingent emergence and dominance of the trend of 'historical consciousness' in the two centuries that separate them.

modern or classical, constructs the 'future' as nothing other than the perpetuation of the status quo. The future in its proper sense (the time of another historical block) is "something to be produced." This occurs in "political" or "minority cinema," which Deleuze fashions after the model of "minor literature," conjointly developed with Félix Guattari in their reading of Kafka (Deleuze 1995, 215–24; see also Deleuze and Guattari 1986). Far from being "presupposed already there," the future, like "the presence of the people" whom minority cinema addresses, is "what is missing." The function of minority cinema, therefore, consists in "contributing to the invention of a people" and a time that "no longer exist, or not yet" (Deleuze 1995, 217, 216). In linguistic terms, minor cinema is "a cinema of the speech-act," a performative rather than constative cinema, meant to effect the emergence of another social reality which either existed in the past or will emerge at some future point (222).[11]

There would be no problem with Deleuze's model if it were not for the fact that one of the side-effects of the pantheism of value in secular capitalism is that once any *telos* is inserted within diachrony, it is doomed to be eternally deferred—that is, never to happen. Diachrony is not any random illusion, but a central, secular disciplining mechanism whose function is precisely to prevent any future as the realization of a state other than the status quo. The eternal law of secular diachrony is, to appropriate one of Althusser's famous lines, that the final moment or the future never arrives. This fact is due to the capitalist phenomenon known as "credit," which is not an exceptional case but the essence of all capital, since, as Karatani puts it, capital "is itself already a kind of credit," as becomes evident in the fact that "a bank note (or a check) is credit" (1995, 177). Indeed, credit opens from within the time of value the door to diachrony, but its very nature is precisely the postponement of the final settling of accounts.

Due to the economic-semantic homology, secular reason, too, puts the final moment also on credit. Just as the myth of "original sin" as the genealogical cause of capitalism reveals to us the eternal law of circulation-time, it is the myth purporting to explain the genealogy of the secular conception of the 'end of time' that reveals the eternal law of secular diachrony as eternal deferment.

In Hans Blumenberg's succinct recapitulation of the myth in question, historical time conceived as a continuity toward an end is the secular residue of a theocratic idea: the Last Judgment. At a certain point in history, Gnosticism concluded that if the universe was, according to Christian Neoplatonism, divided into two parts (ideal heavens and inferior earthly simulacrum), then divinity must also be divided into two entities: the redeemer who "has never had anything to do with this world," and the demiurge or creator of the earthly world. The demiurge thereby became "the principle of badness, the opponent of the transcendent God of salvation," just as the demiurge's creation, the "cosmos," became "the system of a fall." As a result, Blumenberg concludes, "the downfall of the world becomes the critical process of

---

11. The distinction between constative and performative functions of representation originates in speech act theory (see Austin 1975). Briefly put, by constative function of representation (whether in language or image) one refers to its 'passive' function to describe or constate a reality assumed to be already given. By contrast, the performative function of representation is its ability to change and produce reality as it describes it.

final salvation, the dissolution of the demiurge's illegitimate creation" (1985, 128–9). The destruction of the world became the logical requirement of Neoplatonic theodicy. Ignoring Neoplatonism, however, the world stubbornly continued to exist, and the sole way to cover up this inconsistency was to attribute the world's continuing existence to a delay of the Last Judgment as the manifestation of a merciful God-Redeemer who was willing to satisfy the human prayer for postpone-ment of the destruction of the world. The difference between the presecular and the secular conceptions of the Last Judgment lies in the shift of historical consciousness from "prayer ... for the early coming of the Lord" to prayer "for postponement of the end" (131).

In other words, if the "transcendent God of salvation" appears to act incon-sistently and not destroy the world as he should, it is due to humans' own fault since they are the ones who implore him to postpone it. If Blumenberg sees in the inconsistency of theodicy the very cause that led to the collapse of theocracy and the process of secularization, it is because his 'diachronic' narrative is pronounced from the perspective of an already secular place of enunciation: if theodicy is inconsistent, humans themselves must take responsibility for it; they must provide a fantasmatic surplus that makes the Gnostic conclusion appear consistent even as the world continues to exist. Stated in Lacan's more universalizing terms: if theocratic feudalism is replaced with secular capitalism, it is because the subjects' surplus-enjoyment began to adjoin itself to the truth of the Other. The circularity of this myth may not capture the genealogy of secular reason but it teaches us that the moment the surplus begins to adjoin itself to the truth of the Other, the future end ceases to arrive.

The capitalist discourse is equipped with mechanisms that eliminate finitude in diachronic time. Value knows only two temporal modes: *circulation-time* and *credit-time,* the diachrony of an eternally deferred end.

In this regard, it can be said that, while Deleuze placed his hope for another historical block in the wrong place, or rather, time, deconstruction got it right. Its prominent proponent, Jacques Derrida, indeed praised the "specular circle" with its "distant hunt," the "hunt *for* distance," which takes place in a "*long time,*" "the time of *this distance hunt*" for a *telos* that is "nothing other than this ghost hunt, but nothing but this singular nothing that a ghost remains" (1994, 140–1). Derrida is undoubtedly right to declare that the *telos* of any diachrony is a "ghost," but one must also inquire into the desire motivating his celebration of ghosts. Indeed, if you desire to turn Marx into a "specter," the "nothing that a ghost remains," one of the most effective ways to do so (besides expecting credit-time to come to a rest, whether in the fashion of stage theory or in the Deleuzean mode) is by celebrating the "ghost hunt" for the future.

Recapitulating, there can be no "minor" conception of the future within a history cast in diachronic terms. The so-called future is another present, yet unrealized block whose structure can be articulated only through its formal difference from the given past and present blocks. Not only the perpetuation of the status quo but also its replacement by another block are effects of the crystal-image: the former its realized effect, the latter its unrealized, *desired* effect.

The temporal relation between any other block that could possibly replace the capitalist block and the latter forms itself a crystal-image. The old Master, while being other than the modern Master, is his presupposed past in the crystal-image that articulates the relation between past feudalism and present capitalism. This is Marx's point about the myth of the genealogy of capitalism: once in the block of value, 'past' or 'future' other blocks can be conceived only in terms of synchronic immanent causality. By the same token, since past and future are contemporaneous with the present, a really minor cultural production, including theory and the analysis of culture, must speak from the place of enunciation of this unrealized other block *here and now*. Indeed, even if Deleuze severs the future from the crystal-image, what he nevertheless seeks in the filmic examples he selects as representative of a minor cinema is the articulation of another reality here and now (regardless of whether one would agree that his actual choice of examples meets this criterion).

Killing Time

What, then, one might ask, is the problem with Negri and Hardt's neo-Spinozist model of absolute immanence, which indeed articulates the future as, at least formally, always already present? There is a difference between the *reduction* of the other block *to* the present block, and *another* block that exists (unrealized) *simultaneously* with the present block. In the first case, the surplus is always assimilated by capital and 'objective knowledge'.

To exemplify this difference, let us turn to the final pages of Hardt and Negri's *Empire*. In Empire—that is, in our present global and informatized state of late capitalism, as Hardt and Negri write, there is no way to differentiate "work time from leisure time" since "the proletariat produces in all its generality everywhere all day" (2000, 403). This ceaseless state of production, as well as all other major phenomena of postmodern capitalism proper (the increasing "mass migrations" of the "multitude," "necessary for production," and the "hybridization of human and machine"), are to be celebrated as the signs of the multitude's triumph over the Empire for, far from being imposed and governed by the latter, they are the very manifestation of "the spontaneity of the multitude's movements" (398, 400, 405). The movement of capital and its *telos* are "the spontaneity of the multitude's movements" and the "telos of the multitude" (407). No need for revolution or any form of resistance, since the future has already arrived as the historical stage of the Empire.

If anything needs to be changed, these are only few points concerning legislation, which come to constitute Hardt and Negri's communist manifesto. The latter consists of the demands for (1) "The Right to Global Citizenship," so that 'illegal' immigrant labor is officially recognized as legal; (2) "The Right to a Social Wage," so that everybody contributing to production—including its aspects of reproduction (e.g., services) and unproduction (since unemployment is also presupposed for capitalism to sustain itself)—be equally paid; and (3) "The Right to Reappropriation," so that the multitude have control over the means of production (which today have become the technology of information) that are anyway already "increasingly integrated into the minds and bodies of the multitude" (396, 401, 403, 407).

Regarding the right to reappropriation, one might wonder how the multitude can have control over something that is anyway already "increasingly integrated into [their] minds and bodies." And what would global, informatized capitalism welcome more than the legitimization, offered by Hardt and Negri's advocacy of the right to a social wage, of the presently actual return to the pre–five-eight-hour-day-week postmodern mode of production? Since only leisure time can be killed, and the latter no longer exists, Hardt and Negri implicitly argue that time can no longer be legitimately killed. A fortiori, as the analysis here shows, time can no longer be legitimately killed because capitalism has already killed time—both the time in which people can kill time, and the time in which they can also kill, be killed, and die. The eternal laws of value postulate that all that remain in legitimacy are the circulation- and credit-times of exchangeable and immortal values—that not even unemployment and leisure escape their divine force. Similarly, the 'right' to "global citizenship" only serves the sustenance of capital, reflecting the needs of present global and informatized capital.

In truth, like the 'freedom of the individual' and that of 'expression' before them, these are the very 'rights' that the present legislation, as soon as it catches up with the pace of global, informatized capital itself, will be more than happy to grant. This might occur only after violent interventions or peacefully, but in either case, at the end we shall still be in global, informatized capitalism—perhaps also at the dawn of a new stage of capitalism, but still capitalism. This, however, Hardt and Negri call "*communism*." If true, then communism and capitalism coincide as the totalized imperialism of value.

Might the pantheism of value necessarily entail the total subsumption of everything under its reign, so that even what intends to oppose its empire must always in truth serve it? Is Gramsci's *transformismo* the inevitable destiny of the Left?[12] Have 'free time' and all forms of leisure's enjoyment become indeed irrevocably impossible, nothing other than a necessary part of production?

No, simply because the more totalizing the reign of value and the elimination of enjoyment become, the more they foster enjoyment of sense, and the latter opens the back door to sensation—and, along with it, mortality. The more value makes finitude impossible within its temporal categories, the more mortality returns on the level of the real. This is where the realm of biopolitics begins.

---

12. Originating in the 1870s, *transformismo* is the concept Gramsci adopted and extended in the years 1931–2, in his *Prison Notebooks*, to describe the state of bourgeois hegemony in Italy. In *transformismo*, opposition and the possibility of undermining power, far from being real or effective, are ostensible and effectively absorbed by the hegemonic groups. The main referent in Gramsci's mind was the transformism of leftist individuals or groups who go over to the center or right, as when ex-leftists or -anarchists become members of conservative parties (see Gramsci 1971, particularly 52–120, 128–30; for the Italian original, see Gramsci 1975, notebook 8, par. 36, 962–3). But the term is also used to designate not so much the explicit transformism of leftist individuals or groups into more conservative ones, but, rather, a covert—including possibly unconscious—transformism in which individuals or groups, as the historian Norman Stone puts it, "talk left and act right" (1984, 45). (For a productive application of the term to contemporary politics, see Waite 1996, particularly 365–72.)

Acknowledgements

My gratitude goes to David F. Ruccio for his general support, and to Yahya M. Madra for his profound engagement with the arguments advanced in my essay, which led me to pursue further their logical conclusions.

References

Althusser, L. 1971. *Lenin and philosophy and other essays*. Trans. B. Brewster. New York: Monthly Review Press.

——, 1996. *For Marx*. Trans. B. Brewster. New York: Vintage.

Arendt, H. 1978. *The life of the mind*. New York: Harcourt Brace Jovanovich.

Austin, J. L. 1975. *How to do things with words*. Ed. J. O. Urmson and M. Sbisà. Cambridge, Mass.: Harvard University Press.

Benjamin, W. 1969. *Illuminations*. Trans. H. Zohn, ed. H. Arendt. New York: Schocken.

——. 1977. *The origin of German tragic drama*. Trans. J. Osborne. London: Verso.

Bentham, J. 1932. *Theory of fictions*. Ed. C. K. Ogden. London: Kegan Paul, Trench, Trubner & Company.

Blumenberg, H. 1985. *The legitimacy of the modern age*. Trans. R. M. Wallace. Cambridge, Mass.: MIT Press.

Burke, K. 1970. *The rhetoric of religion: Studies in logology*. Berkeley: University of California Press.

Copjec, J. 1994. *Read my desire: Lacan against the historicists*. Cambridge, Mass.: MIT Press.

Deleuze, G. 1985. *Kant's critical philosophy: The doctrine of the faculties*. Trans. H. Tomlinson and B. Habberjam. Minneapolis: University of Minnesota Press.

——. 1995. *Cinema 2: The time—image*. Trans. H. Tomlinson and R. Galeta. Minneapolis: University of Minnesota Press.

Deleuze, G., and F. Guattari. 1986. *Kafka: Toward a minor literature*. Trans. D. Polan. Minneapolis: University of Minnesota Press.

——. 1994. *Specters of Marx: The state of the debt, the work of mourning, and the New International*. Trans. P. Kamuf. New York: Routledge.

Descartes, R. 1968. *Discourse on method and The meditations*. Trans. F. E. Sutcliffe. London: Penguin.

Foucault, M. 1970. *The order of things: An archaeology of the human sciences*. New York: Vintage.

Freud, S. 1999. *Gesammelte Werke*. Ed. A. Freud. Frankfort: Fischer.

Gramsci, A. 1971. *Selections from prison notebooks*. Trans. and ed. Q. Hoare and G. Nowell-Smith. Cambridge, Mass.: Harvard University Press.

——. 1975. *Quaderni del carcere*. 4 vols. Ed. V. Gerratana. Turin.

Hardt, M., and A. Negri 2000. *Empire*. Cambridge, Mass.: Harvard University Press.

Holland, E. 1998. Spinoza and Marx. *Cultural Logic* 2.1 (Fall).

Jameson, F. 1991. *Postmodernism, or, The cultural logic of late capitalism*. Durham, N.C.: Duke University Press.

Kafka, F. 1979. The Great Wall of China. In *The basic Kafka*, 66–80. New York: Washington Square Press.

Kant, I. 1977. *Prolegomena to any future metaphysics that will be able to come forward as science*. Trans. J. Ellington. Indianapolis: Hacket.

——. 1998. *Critique of pure reason*. Trans. and ed. P. Guyer and A. W. Wood. New York: Cambridge University Press.

Karatani, K. 1995. *Architecture as metaphor: Language, number, money*. Trans. S. Kohso, ed. M. Speaks. Cambridge, Mass.: MIT Press.

——, 2003. *Transcritique: On Kant and Marx*. Trans. S. Kohso. Cambridge, Mass.: MIT Press.

Kordela, A. K. 2007. *Şurplus (Spinoza-Lacan)*. New York: State University of New York Press.

Lacan, J. 1977. *Écrits: A selection*. Trans. A. Sheridan. New York: W. W. Norton.

——. 1981. *The four fundamental concepts of psychoanalysis*. Trans. A. Sheridan, ed. J.-A. Miller. New York: W. W. Norton.

——. 1991. *Le Séminaire. Livre XVII: L'envers de la psychanalyse, 1969–1970*. Ed. J.-A. Miller. Paris: Seuil.

——. 1992. *Book VII. The ethics of psychoanalysis, 1959–1960*. Trans. D. Porter, ed. J.-A. Miller. New York: W. W. Norton.

——. 1993. *Book III: The psychoses, 1955–56*. Trans. R. Grigg, ed. J.-A. Miller. New York: W. W. Norton.

——. 1998. *Book XX. Encore, 1972–1973: On feminine sexuality; The limits of love and knowledge*. Trans. B. Fink, ed. J.-A. Miller. New York: W. W. Norton.

Macherey, P. 1979. *Hegel ou Spinoza*. Paris: François Maspero.

Mannoni, O. 1969. *Clefs pour l'imaginaire ou l'autre scène*. Paris: Seuil.

Marx, K. 1990. *Capital: A critique of political economy*. Vol. 1. Trans. B. Fowkes. London: Penguin.

——. 1993. *Grundrisse: Foundations of the critique of political economy (Rough draft)*. Trans. M. Nicolaus. London: Penguin Books and *New Left Review*.

Norton, B. 1995. Late capitalism and postmodernism: Jameson/Mantel. In *Marxism in the postmodern age: Confronting the new world order*, ed. A. Callari, S. Cullenberg and C. Biewener. New York: Guilford.

Saussure, F. de. 1966. *Course in general linguistics*. Trans. R. Harris, ed. C. Bally et al. London: Duckworth.

Simmel, G. 1990. *The Philosophy of money*. 2d ed. Trans. T. Bottomore and D. Frisby from a first draft by K. Mengelberg, ed. D. Frisby. London: Routledge.

Sohn-Rethel, A. 1978. *Intellectual and manual labor*. Trans. M. Sohn-Rethel. London: Macmillan.

Spinoza, B. de. 1985. *The collected works of Spinoza*. Trans. and ed. E. Curley. Princeton, N.J.: Princeton University Press.

Stone, N. 1984. *Europe transformed, 1878–1919*. Cambridge, Mass.: Harvard University Press.

Vaihinger, H. 1924. *The philosophy of "as-if."* 2d ed. Trans. C. K. Ogden. New York: Harper and Row.

Waite, G. 1996. *Nietzsche's corps/e: Aesthetics, politics, prophecy, or, The spectacular technoculture of everyday life*. Durham, N.C.: Duke University Press.

Žižek, S. 1989. *The sublime object of ideology*. London: Verso.

—— 1991. *For they know not what they do: Enjoyment as a political factor*. London: Verso.

——. 1996. The fetish of the party. In *Lacan, politics, aesthetics*, ed. W. Apollon and R. Feldstein, 3–29. New York: State University of New York Press.

——, ed. 1992. *Everything you always wanted to know about Lacan (but were afraid to ask Hitchcock)*. London: Verso.

RETHINKING MARXISM   VOLUME 18   NUMBER 4   (OCTOBER 2006)

Remarx

Interests and the Political Terrain of Time

Geoff Mann

Confronting conservatism in U.S. politics, especially within the working class, demands a rethinking of the concept of "interests" that underlies contemporary Left critiques of the last two federal elections. Plumbing the depths of "interests" or class "interest" will provide little analytical or political purchase without some recognition of the temporal orientation of working-class conservatism. If the Left's interests are only "about" the future, we cede political terrain absolutely fundamental to working-class cultural politics (i.e., "values"): the struggle over the past, of which nostalgia is perhaps the best evidence.

Key Words: Interests, Time, Conservatism, U.S. Politics

VOTE, *n*. The instrument and symbol of a freeman's power to make a fool of himself and a wreck of his country.

—Ambrose Bierce, *The Devil's Dictionary*

The elections of November 2000 and 2004 have thrown into dramatic relief the conservatism that dominates white working-class political life in the United States. While these developments are by no means historyless, the extent to which white workers appear to have accelerated into a right turn has not only left the Democratic party slack-jawed, but also has exposed some inconsistencies in the Left's critical apparatus—inconsistencies that it seems were even willfully obscured by Bill Clinton's nominal status as a Democrat. Any remaining faith in the belief that "you can't treat people like that" now stands on very unstable ground, for it appears that you can treat people like that.

George W. Bush's election, not to mention the Republicans' triumph in states like West Virginia where theory suggests this should not happen, has robbed the Left of a big part of the political and moral legitimacy it has always claimed in speaking for the disempowered. In an effort to extricate ourselves (if I may speak for the Left) from a web of confusion woven with little more than sorrow and anger, the persistent political critique we claim as our ethical and political bread-and-butter has found some new energy, but it has also lashed out less discriminately. Now, many of us are

ISSN 0893-5696 print/1475-8059 online/06/040565-20
© 2006 Association for Economic and Social Analysis
DOI: 10.1080/08935690600901228

Routledge
Taylor & Francis Group

embittered not only with George Bush's junta, but also with U.S. working-class whites. We may not always be willing to admit the latter—it seems to contradict our commitment to "the people"—but we perform it every time someone snickers remorsefully over the front page of Britain's *Daily Mirror* on 4 November 2004 ("How Can 59,054,087 People Be So Dumb?") and every time someone apologizes to non-Americans for the election (and especially when they mutter defensively, "*I* didn't vote for him"). What we are saying is that those 59,054,087 people are stupid, at least the ones who aren't wealthy, and they embarrass us (both because we do not want to be associated with them, and because they prove us wrong). We ask, "Why do workers vote against their interests?" And we respond, increasingly, with the rearticulation of a critique that had been hiding its face until recently, even if it never really went away: false consciousness.

I am as troubled as anyone by the contemporary condition of politics in the United States, but my purpose in offering this intervention is less to assess the accuracy of the false consciousness claim (i.e., "working-class voters do not understand what is good for them") than to reflect upon its foundational place in Left political discourse under Bush. The problem is not merely with the arrogance, and the oft-noted political and theoretical weaknesses of the "false consciousness" argument. Rather, in light of what are surely important diagnoses of progressive political paralysis, what I want to suggest is that while "they don't get it" explanations are a product of important intuitions, there is more rigorous critical work to be done—at least insofar as that work might elicit the political responses for which it calls. And I think a crucial step in this work is the specification of the "it" the U.S. working class needs to "get," for I am not sure we (the radical critics) know "it," either. In any event, I am fairly certain that whatever "it" looks like, it is not just "you are getting robbed of your hard-earned wages," and will emerge only through reinvigoration of a praxis that does not snicker. A furrowed brow is fine. So too, I think, is irony, but irony really *laughs*.

That said, what follows cannot pretend to provide a "solution," the finality of which suggests it is probably the wrong thing to look for anyway. Instead, I want to argue that some significant part of the critical difficulty lies in the very notion of "interest," and perhaps more particularly in "class interest" (a phrase some say has no referent [Laclau and Mouffe 1985; Reddy 1987]). We need to take up this often tacit problematic of scholarship on the cultural politics of capitalism. For, although more frequently noted in its absence than elaborated in any positive sense, a theory of worker interests nonetheless underwrites all work on class and labor politics. Indeed, it is implicit in every emancipatory critique of labor's subordination under capitalism, in every liberal or utilitarian defense of status quo inequities, and in every attempt by the Left to understand Novembers 2000 and 2004.

The best-known answer to the "against their interests" question is Thomas Frank's fascinating *What's the Matter with Kansas?* (2004), but there are several other compelling examples, among them Slavoj Žižek's contributions to the *London Review of Books* (2004a, 2004b), the essays of Jefferson Cowie and others in the *New Labor Forum* (2004), and Serge Halimi in *Le Monde diplomatique* (2004). In each of these instances, the writers present arguments broadly similar in contour: U.S. workers contradict a Weberian "economic interest" indicating instead some cultural or political affinity, an affinity that is definitively not an "interest" in the old "against their interests" sense.

The range of explanations for the results of the two Novembers offered by the authors just mentioned demonstrates that a critical rethinking of "interest" could go in several directions. We could, for example, follow Laclau and Mouffe, rejecting the concept since it "lacks any theoretical basis whatsoever, and involves little more than an arbitrary attribution of interests, by the analyst, to a certain category of social agents" (1985, 83). Or, we could stretch the concept of interest to encompass a range of desires and needs much broader than those accommodated by Weber's "economic." Alternatively, we might dig into interests, to try to clarify what is at stake, to ask, "What are interests?" I offer the remaining paragraphs as a contribution to the latter pursuit.

In *The German Ideology*, Marx argues that big industry "makes for the worker not only the relation to the capitalist, but labour itself, unbearable" (Marx and Engels 1998, 82). Unbearable: this is a key element at the core of Marx's conception of the working-class subject. He cannot mean the material relations are unbearable in the physical sense, for the argument of the subsistence wage—which Marx never meant in a purely physiological sense—is not what is at stake here. Nor, certainly, does he mean "unbearable" in a beyond-the-threshold-of-toleration sense, for people go on bearing this unbearability day in and day out, just as they did when Marx was writing. The liberal-individualist suggestion that, from this perspective, the labor/capital antagonism has not proved as unbearable as Marx thought, entirely misses the point. The persistent silence of some "silent majority" represents neither indifference nor consent.

Rather, what is at stake are the conditions that make the unbearable bearable, or produce ways of masking its unbearability (which would seem to challenge the very notion in the first place). In any event, the unbearable proves fluid and ideological. As such, Marx's largely unstated liberal theory of workers' objective interests under capitalism (true freedom) and his argument for the irreducibly ideological content of the "unbearable"—a combination that underwrites his theory of justice, his theory of history, and his political theory and activism—leave us without much purchase on the political substance of interest. Certainly, we know that the kernel of emancipatory energy that presumably lies within us all is subdued without the "it" that Ohioans or Kansans need to "get," but that "it" seems as distant as ever.

We know, too, that the "unbearable" relations that constitute much social life under capitalism are in fact bearable (that is Marx's point), and that the subject who can bear capitalism is, by definition, the worker. His or her constitution as subject is dependent upon a field of "material" interest that "in the last instance" determines the shifting ideological terrain of bearability. But even these presumably relatively straightforward "material" interests are slippery things to confront. To begin with—and this is by no means a strictly intellectual problem—it is very difficult to specify what produces an interest, where the tracing backward or digging down into an interest might "end up." We commonly understand interests as representing or as being produced by desires or needs: we are interested, for example, in wealth accumulation because we seek or need social status or long-term security. But we can perform the same disinterment with these, understood as interests: why do we need status or security? One can only imagine that this process would eventually lead us to something like a genetically encoded competitiveness, a Nietzschean will to power, or Freudian unconscious drives (all of which, in their turn to naturalization and universalization, are basically positivist, quasi-biological explanations). This is not to say these are necessarily dead ends, but any explanation of interests that "ends up" without making claims about "human nature"—avoiding what Sartre called "biological materialism" (1976, 217)—proves very tricky.

For instance, we may try to work back (e.g., Weber) or down (e.g., Lévi-Strauss) from what we call "interests" to some "hierarchy of needs," and found them ultimately on food, water, shelter, and love. This indeed may be where we could finally "end up," but it would not contribute very much to an understanding of political struggle and negotiation, let alone the analysis of cultural and political economy in North America where, at least in comparison with many other parts of the world, these basic needs may be constant but are nonetheless generally met (with perhaps the exception of love). This is not in any way to suggest that the struggle to provide all North Americans with the services, shelter, and sustenance to allow dignified and enjoyable lives is not desperately necessary; rather, I mean only to suggest that there is so much social life piled on top of these basic needs that asserting their fundamental causal originality leaves us pretty much where we started, trying to deal with everything that stands between our everyday lives and histories and those "needs."

In the face of these theoretical difficulties, which are also and inevitably political challenges, a "poststructural" turn has proven very attractive to Left critique. Around that corner, we find interests emerging from subjectivities that are neither natural nor universal, but products of power, history, language, codes, desires, and so on. This is a crucial turn and one that we must seriously consider, but with hesitation, so as not to throw the baby out with the bathwater: we cannot, I think, lose sight of ideology, the very fabric of cultural politics. Yet, the risks of doing so are substantial. Poststructuralism's affinity for psychoanalytic theory smuggles in the seeds of what is basically a "desire-rationality," a Freudian addition to the Weberian typology of motivation (ends-rationality, value-rationality, and instinct).

The debilitating problems this poses are perhaps best illustrated by one of the most influential takes on subjectivity in recent years, Deleuze and Guattari's *Capitalism and Schizophrenia* volumes (1983, 1987). Deleuze and Guattari assert that interests and needs are posited by desire (1983, 27; Foucault and Deleuze 1977, 214–5). Yet that does not get us out of this analytical knot since desire, for them, serves the same functions as need in older, more explicitly biological or evolutionary models. We, and they, are left with the same problems with which we began, redefined with what might be called a "beat" flair: where does desire come from? Deleuze and Guattari tell us it comes from, and is, unconscious; unconscious desire posits our interests in consciousness. But what is the unconscious here if not a theoretical trapdoor: "human nature" by another name? Instead of establishing some basis for the understanding of interests, let alone for politics, they found interest where we cannot go (the unconscious), then give it an ontogenetic status that basically defies theorization. As Gayatri Spivak has pointed out (1988, 273), they explicitly refuse a *politics* of interest—that is, ideology—placing its dynamics out of reflective reach by force of will alone, and offer an explanation of the subject as the "residual" of desire (Deleuze and Guattari 1983, 26, 40–1). What remains is little more than a theory of "false unconsciousness."

Keeping a politics of interest in the United States in focus, then, seems to me to demand both a return to the question that founds the diverse Marxian and social democratic approaches of Halimi and Žižek, Frank and Cowie—namely, does the concept of interest help explain what makes capitalism so bearable, even welcome, despite its "unbearability"?—and a recognition that interest is not only neither natural nor universal. It is also, and perhaps most importantly, not necessarily prior to politics.

If these are indeed meaningful critical premises, then the answer to the question, "Is interest a product of 'needs,' psychic or material?" is "Perhaps not." Perhaps the only meaning we can salvage for "interest" is the interest in having *an* interest. Perhaps interests represent, or are a product of, a struggle-search for political subjectivity or agency, an endeavor that is by definition never complete. Such a conception points toward the political (which is not to say fully intentional) construction of subject positions; in other words, one does not choose and construct one's subjecthood or subjection. Rather, social roles and spaces to which individuals or groups are allocated interact with the agency of these (and other) individuals and groups. The polyvalence of race, which can be simultaneously embraced solidarity and assigned stigma, is an excellent example of how this might work itself out in a particular time and place.

We might then understand this kind of overdetermined and ultimately unrealizable struggle-search as the substance of a political agency that is not so much a means to the realization of other, more "immediate" historical and material interests, but as, in fact, interest itself. I think such a conception is certainly more in tune with working-class political formation, which proves so fluid, so historically specific, so dynamic. The problem of the conservative or quiescent working class in the contemporary capitalist United States, then, might not be so much one of the repression, the strategic obfuscation, or the misapprehension of (white) workers' "true" interests. Instead, the problem could be the almost overwhelming difficulty facing the determination of a noncapitalist—that is, revolutionary—political subject by interests that are never fully articulated: indeed, whose interests may be indeterminate, not yet articulable, by definition. This is the inescapable problem of ideology, one among many reasons to wonder how complete the Left's victory might have (already) been if we could jumble history's trajectory, and put the future first.

If interests have a meaning for, and within, this inescapability, I believe it is here in the constant presence of the "not yet" that they can provide some purchase on the conservatism of the white working class. Politics, at least as ordinarily conceived in academic literature and everyday discourse, are unreservedly future-oriented, even when they are "about" the past. "Interests" are inextricably bound up in this political future-dynamic. Interests are about the future, and insofar as an individual or collective agent's actions are seen to be either congruent or conflicting with their attributed or claimed "interests," those actions are evaluated according to the degree to which we expect them to hinder or abet the confluence of "interest" and social life *in the future*.

But if the working-class supporters of Bush are, as we say, "conservative," we must take the temporal orientation of this politics seriously. Indeed, as the fascinating work of people like Aaron Fox (2004) and Kathleen Stewart (1996) has demonstrated so compellingly, the characterization of white working-class politics in the "red-state" Bush heartland as conservative, or even "reactionary," is grossly imprecise, and in desperate need of elaboration. Their accounts of contemporary rural Texas and West Virginia give analytical substance to a "world in the image of life as it was" (however imagined), a political culture that is constituted primarily as "a strong claim on the present in the key of nostalgia" (Fox 2004, 42, 319). This "obsession" with the past, and its supposed moral superiority, produces an "interest" that is by definition not "progressive," but precisely antifutural.

Against this background, it seems that either the entire conceptual apparatus of interest is not helpful, since it is essentially looking the wrong way, and/or working-class interests are an interest in the past, or at least in a fundamental antipathy to the future-as-progress, leading to what is basically a desire to slow down time. The country songs that fill the air of millions of American workplaces speak this desire more or less explicitly. This temporal orientation, this participation in time—which helped make Fukuyama's (1992) declaration of "the end of history" a cause for celebration—runs against the most basic assumptions of Left politics and temporal perspectives, which, in even their most patient, Gramscian, terrain-shifting mani-festation, still constitute a quasi-panicked scramble up the scree slope of history. The unfortunate temptation to frame this politics of history as "antipolitics," to which I have succumbed myself (Mann 2003), arises from this often unreflective obsession with the future, and its associated faith in the ultimate recoverability of interest-to-be-realized.

And perhaps more significantly, I think, it limits our conception of what "counts" as an appropriately "political" object. If so, then the question, "why does the working class vote against its interests?" is based upon a misconception of the content of contemporary workers' politics. If interests are about having an interest, then Bush voters did not articulate an interest in the future the Left heralds, but an interest in the past, an interest in when they (believe they) had an interest. There is absolutely nothing false or "stupid" in that.

Moreover, this is to say little of the extent to which such a question hinders our own self-critique as scholars of the Left, and severely limits our capacity to understand that the politics of the "New American Century," with its eerie fascist undertones, is simultaneously, like other fascisms, a politics of history. What is at stake is not merely the old question of "he who writes the history books" (the "he" is intentional here). This is not just about the selective construction of the past. What is at stake, rather, is what politics can do to and for history. I think it is fair to say that the greatest achievements and the most significant limitations of the Left-radical project have resulted from a "progressive" view of history, and consequent attempts to wrest control of the train of history and create a future that redeems time from the injustices of the past. In contrast, U.S. conservatism's declensionist narrative, like other fascisms with which I am familiar, politicizes history in a very different way. The object is not so much a return to some real or mythical past—in this case, perhaps, to a something like the underbelly of an episode from *Happy Days*—which (even fascists know) is beyond reach. Instead, the task of the project of the future is to affirm that *Happy Days* past, however mythical, to sound its echoes. The Bush administration's mourning for the good ol' days is in this sense more than mere propagandist recruitment; it is a substantive alternative to a politics of time that condemns the past as an aberration. Repeal *Roe* v. *Wade*, reinscribe "family values," roll back civil rights protections, reinforce the "right to work": this is more than nostalgia; it is a politics of redemption, one no less powerful for being manufactured, or for being beholden to "the way we never were" (Coontz 2000).

For how we think about interest, which is how we think about politics, the challenge seems to lie in the degree to which we can radicalize what I have called the struggle-search for political agency that constitutes the politics of interest in an always ideologically saturated social context. At a conceptual level, this would almost certainly entail the kind of counterhegemonic terrain production that Gramsci suggested and practiced. It may also mean out-Gramsci-ing Gramsci, recognizing that the transformation to which this process leads is not only gradual but unending, if "true freedom" is indeed where we will "end up." But just as significantly, we must openly acknowledge that the production of the "new" terrain, of radical histories and interests therein—through the diverse exemplary efforts, for example, of people like Joe Strummer or Mike Davis—is no less ideological than the power it escapes. I do not believe we are very good at this, at turning our critique upon ourselves. If we could do that, it might elicit an acknowledgment of the power and prevalence of loss, regret, nostalgia, and the depth of mourning for what used to be. We might even discover ways to celebrate an everyday working-class past, outside the distracting if important heroisms of the Industrial Workers of the World or Woody Guthrie, without snickering.

References

Bierce, A. 1958. *The devil's dictionary*. Mount Vernon: The Peter Pauper Press.

Coontz, S. 2000. *The way we never were: American families and the nostalgia trap*. New York: Basic Books.

Cowie, J. 2004. From hard-hats to the NASCAR dads. *New Labor Forum* 13 (3): 9–17.

Deleuze, G., and F. Guattari. 1983. *Anti-Oedipus*. Trans. R. Hurley, M. Seem, and H. R. Lane. Minneapolis: University of Minnesota Press.

——. 1987. *A thousand plateaus*. Trans. B. Massumi. Minneapolis: University of Minnesota Press.

Foucault, M., and G. Deleuze. 1977. Intellectuals and power. In *Language, counter-memory, practice*, trans. D. Bouchard and S. Simon, ed. D. Bouchard. Ithaca, N.Y.: Cornell University Press.

Fox, A. 2004. *Real country: Music and language in working class culture*. Durham, N.C.: Duke University Press.

Frank, T. 2004. *What's the matter with Kansas? How conservatives won the heart of America*. New York: Metropolitan Books.

Fukuyama, F. 1992. *The end of history and the last man*. New York: Avon.

Halimi, S. 2004. What's the matter with West Virginia? *Le Monde diplomatique*, October.

Laclau, E., and C. Mouffe. 1985. *Hegemony and socialist strategy: Toward a radical democratic politics*. New York: Verso.

Mann, G. 2003. "Discrimination costs you dough": Innocent identity and the anti-politics of race. *Political Power and Social Theory* 16: 105–39.

Marx, K., and F. Engels. 1998. *The German ideology*. New York: Prometheus Books.

Reddy, W. 1987. *Money and liberty in modern Europe: A critique of historical understanding*. Cambridge: Cambridge University Press.

Sartre, J.-P. 1976. *Critique of dialectical reason*. Vol. 1, *Theory of practical ensembles*. Trans. A. Sheridan-Smith. London: New Left Books.

Spivak, G. S. 1988. Can the subaltern speak? In *Marxism and the interpretation of culture*, ed. C. Nelson and L. Grossberg. Urbana: University of Illinois Press.

Stewart, K. 1996. *A space by the side of the road: Cultural poetics in an "other" America*. Princeton, N.J.: Princeton University Press.

Žižek, S. 2004a. Over the rainbow. *London Review of Books*, 4 November.

———. 2004b. Hooray for Bush! *London Review of Books*, 2 December.

Marx's Learning Process: Against Correcting Marx with Hegel

Wolfgang Fritz Haug
Translated by Eric Canepa, reworked by the author

According to neo-Hegelian readings, Marx's theoretical exposition deteriorates after the Grundrisse. He is said to have sacrificed his (Hegelian) dialectical method on the altar of popularization. In arguing against such readings, this paper interprets Marx's writings as always a "work in progress" in which real advances are achieved. The author stresses the high stakes in these alternative readings. The neo-Hegelian readings tend to disconnect from Marx and Marxism. In contrast, the author articulates and develops the relevance of Marx (and especially his critique of political economy and historical materialist method) to Marxist analysis of contemporary capitalism. He focuses on the special importance of grasping Marx and Marxism as "works in progress" in this time of enormous structural ruptures and transformations.

Key Words: Non-Hegelian Dialectics, Critique of Political Economy, Historical Materialist Method

I have nothing to say, only to show.

—Benjamin, *The Arcades Project*

It is said of the Swabians that they only become "bright" at forty. If we are to believe part of the literature, Karl Marx is an example precisely of the opposite. Soon after he turned forty, his theoretical acumen, it is claimed, went downhill. In the main, it is the Hegelian-oriented interpretations that normally regard as regressive the progress Marx made after the *Grundrisse,* through the first (1867) and second (1872) editions of volume 1 of *Capital* and its French translation (1872–5), and culminating in the *Marginal Notes on Wagner,* since these in fact were steps that, for the most part, led further away from Hegel's speculative dialectics. They claim that, in popularizing, Marx softened the theoretical core of his thinking (see Hoff 2004, 21–7). More particularly, Hans-Georg Backhaus (like Iring Fetscher before him) sees in the reworkings for the second edition of *Capital* a "vulgarization of his value theory produced by Marx himself" (1997, 297). Furthermore, Backhaus transposes to Marx a distinction Marx attributed to Adam Smith, such that Marx is split into a "logical," "esoteric" side, on the one hand, and a "historicizing" and "exoteric" side, on the other (294; similarly, Kurz 2000). The latter is supposed to apply to the Marx who is committed to the labor movement, or tied to so-called "labor-movement Marxism," typically regarded with a certain distaste. Since the collapse of European state socialism of Soviet origin, these critical approaches have, with increasing aggressiveness, been associated with a rejection of any kind of Marxism.

What is at stake here, along with the epistemology of the critique of political economy, is the concept of dialectics. To any attentive reader it is obvious that Marx achieved a change of paradigm, not only in the *Theses on Feuerbach* and, together with Friedrich Engels, *The German Ideology,* but also between the *Contribution to the Critique of Political Economy* (1859) and his last fragment dealing with theoretical foundations, the *Marginal Notes on Wagner.*[1] It is true that Marx did not undertake these shifts with the assertiveness of an explicitly declared break. The changes occur at different times on different levels of methodological understanding, in uneven batches not subjected to systematic reflection, "never producing," as Jacques Bidet observes, "a new version if not because of the insufficiency of the former version in relation to the project he pursues" (2004, 10). As a whole, it is no exaggeration to speak of a paradigm shift that is neither a decline nor an adulterated popularization, but rather, the essential innovation that makes Marx's work "contemporary" even today, understandable as an open theory-praxis project rather than a dogma, and indeed, makes it crucial to the theoretical understanding of the emerging transnational high-tech capitalism.

If it is true that the ever enquiring Marx underwent a learning process, then, for those of us who are affiliated with him, understanding this process is of greatest interest. The first rule for attempting a clarification is: most relevant for us is what Marx *does* as a critic of political economy, and only secondarily, what he *says* about what he does. The operational Marx ranks above the declarative Marx. It goes without saying that, in the space available to us, we can only offer a sketch of an explanatory thesis.

---

1. These notes were dated by the editors of MEW to 1879–80, but by Eike Kopf (1992) to Marx's year of death in 1883.

Popularization

Did Marx sacrifice theoretical rigor to popularization?

Those who argue this refer, for the most part, to changes that Marx undertook for the second edition of volume 1 of *Capital,* in comparison with the first edition. Since I have treated this elsewhere, I will not repeat myself here but will address the popularization argument.[2] Those who introduce it almost always ignore the fact that Marx had already addressed in the first edition the problem that theorization and popularization can conflict with one other. The example is the expression "unpaid labor." It is one of the capitalist basic "categories" in the Marxian sense of "social modes of being, existential determinations" (MEW 42:40) to "pay for labor." When speaking with theoretical strictness Marx explains: (1) Labor possesses no value; rather, it creates value. (2) Wage as the "price of labor" is accordingly an irrational expression for value and price of the commodity labor-power. (3) Exploitation rests on the wageworkers' need to work beyond the point at which their labor has created an equivalent of the wage. (4) On a time scale, this can be registered as a succession of necessary labor and surplus labor. (5) Exploitation thus also takes place when the full value of labor-power is paid for.

Now, to the problem: This presentation conflicts with the categories in which daily practice is expressed. What primarily outrages the labor movement (as also any other social movement) is perceived injustice. That the rich get richer while the poor stay poor or become poorer is understandably experienced as injustice. If labor is paid, this appears to be just; if it is not or is underpaid, this appears to be unjust. In the labor movement, which had to avoid being reduced to its politically and theoretically schooled core, political discourse breaks away from the theoretical. Surplus value, the final source of all profits, is traced back to "unpaid labor." Outrage at bourgeois form speaks bourgeois language.

How does Marx deal with the given political-economic semantics? Does he polemicize against it, as his *Critique of the Gotha Programme* did against ignoring the role of nature and glorifying labor as the sole source of wealth? Not at all. Instead, he adopts the popular way of speaking in his theoretical language. In the first German edition and in the second, which he edited, he has surplus labor = "unpaid labor," surplus value = "from the point of view of its substance, the materialization of unpaid labor time" (MEGA II.5:432, II.6:496; MEW 23:556; Marx 1977, 672). He comments: "unpaid labor / paid labor is only a popular expression for surplus labor / necessary labor." It is as if he wants to soothe his theoretical conscience by using an "as if" construction: If, during necessary labor time, a product is created of the same value as the labor power, it is for the capitalist "as if he had bought the finished product on the market. However, in the period of surplus labor the utilization of labor power represents value for the capitalist, without costing him value compensation. He gets this fluidity of labor power gratis. In this sense, surplus labor can be called unpaid labor." Delio Cantimori's Italian translation cushions the scandal by saying,

---

2. See my article "Historisches/Logisches" in *Historisch-kritisches Wörterbuch des Marxismus* 6, no. 1: 360 ff., as well as the abridged offprint in *Das Argument* 251, 45, no. 3 (2003): 392 f.

instead of the popular "non pagato," "lavoro altrui non retribuito,"[3] while in the English translation overseen by Engels the simple and accurate phrase is "other people's unpaid labor" (MEGA II.9:466). In his Spanish translation, Pedro Scaron has "trabajo ajeno impago" (1975, 2:642), even (as in Cantimori) in italics, as Marx had it in the first edition. "The misconception," Marx says in closing, "to which the formula unpaid labor / paid labor can lead, as if the capitalist paid the labor and not the labor-power, is avoided, after the earlier given development" (672). This is not a theoretically satisfactory explanation; rather, it is a bridge to colloquial language. Here we find Marx's real theoretical sin. Those who accuse him of popularization do not pay attention to this point. On the other hand, precisely at the point where they accuse him of popularization or vulgarization in the sense of a debasement of theory, is where we find decided improvements.

De-Hegelianizing Dialectics

The critique of political economy must not, as often occurs, be conceived as a "system," as if it arose in the time in which philosophers had to construct a system. If there is a system, it is the unsystematic system of the crisis-ridden process of capital itself. Its theoretical critique has to be understood as a research process along with the learning process of the researcher. It is not as if there wouldn't be commentaries by Marx on the paradigm shifts he accomplished in the course of this work in progress. However, the commentaries on method are often too general and sometimes "relatively sketchy, and enigmatic" (Arthur 2002, 9), even misleading. Thus, Marx says, his "dialectical method" is "in its foundations not only different from the Hegelian, but is its direct opposite," and Hegelian dialectics has to be "inverted [umstülpen], in order to discover the rational kernel within the mystical shell." While Hegel is said to have "transformed the thought process ... under the insignia of the idea into an independent subject," in Marx "the ideal" is "nothing but the material world as converted [umgesetzt] and translated in the human brain" (Marx 1977, 102 f., translation corrected; cf. MEW 23:26 f.). Should one, then, as the "direct opposite," transform matter into an independent subject? The assertion that the ideal is the result of the conversion and translation of the material within the human brain misled Plekhanov, in Fundamental Problems of Marxism (1969), into confusing Marx in this regard with Feuerbach. Yet it ought to be clear that the first thesis on Feuerbach categorically forbids deploying a scheme in which thinking without hand and tool and without a social network of activities is directly counterposed to the "material world." The image of "inverting" Hegelian dialectics or "turning it upside down" is actually completely deceptive. It suggests that it would remain intact but be turned around, or, like a glove or a shirt, simply be turned from right to left but remain unchanged in form and texture. In reality, the texture cannot remain here; everything must be disassembled and recomposed according to a completely different algorithm—namely, historical materialism. That Marx in fact

3. "In questo senso il pluslavoro può essere chiamato lavoro non retribuito" (Marx 1964, 582).

does this, at least in the decisive places and at least implicitly, is shown by the analysis of his operational dialectics (cf. Haug 2005).

Sometimes only small traces, which signal a change of terrain, appear in the manifest texts. Where the change remains implicit, gathering these hints becomes a reading for symptoms. A symptom that invites such a reading is found in the second chapter of the French translation of volume 1 of *Capital* by Joseph Roy, whose revision occupied Marx for five years and definitively cost him his linguistic innocence, as Jean-Pierre Lefebvre rightly observes.[4] The "seduction" of thought by language, to which Nietzsche called attention in the 1880s, was suffered for by Marx between 1871 and 1875 in his own chief work. Precisely someone like Marx, who is able to move so masterfully within the idiomatic physiognomy of his mother tongue, tends to regard concepts that seem automatically articulated in language as having been fully established theoretically. Günther Anders asks of us contemporaries that we write in a translatable way. Marx showed a similar concern as he, in his time, came up against the limits of the translatability of his own text. This experience pushed him to sharpen and sometimes even to renew his theoretical thinking. Driven away from his native language (and, by their very nature as self-evident to native speakers, native languages obscure meanings), he had to become clearer about his own moves. Those who, like many German authors, cling to the original version in a linguistically unreflexive way, will experience all clarification as a flattening of meaning. Even for Engels *die ganze Bedeutung*,[5] "the full import" (MEGA II.9:12), appears to be something connected to the German "original"; and where the French translation diverges from it he only sees an "indication of what the author himself was prepared to sacrifice" (MEW 23:37). Such a German myth of origin should not influence international Marxism.[6]

Now to our example. It is found in chapter 2 ("The Exchange Process"). The context is how, in the course of the development of relations of exchange, the dominant determination in each commodity to be a means of exchange, crystallizes into a "money commodity"—indeed, as the "necessary product of the process of exchange" (focusing more on the process involved, the French translation by Marx/ Roy says, "se forme spontanément"). Later we read: "The need to give an external expression to this opposition [of use-value and value] for the purposes of commercial intercourse produces the drive towards an independent form for commodity-value, and [this need] finds neither rest nor peace until [the external expression to this opposition] is finally achieved by the doubling [*Verdopplung*] of the commodity into

4. See his introduction to the French translation of the fourth German edition (Marx 1983).
5. Ben Fowkes translates: "the full impact of the original" (Marx 1977, 110).
6. However, so long as the international Marxist scientific community is lacking in multilingual reflexivity, it is inclined to take national-linguistic particularities for theory. The English translation of *The German Ideology* engenders, as it were, the "individual": where Marx and Engels expressly use the neuter pronoun "es," thus including both genders, the English version has the masculine "he." Jan Rehmann (2000) has traced the hopeless muddle that Marx's *bürgerliche Gesellschaft* (bourgeois society) has caused as "civil society" in English-speaking Marxism.

commodity and money" (my translation; cf. MEW 23:102).[7] Thus, a Hegelian reading, particularly of Marx's analysis of the value-form,[8] attaches itself to what Backhaus (1997, 142) calls the "well-known Hegelian term 'Verdopplung.'" Through "doubling," we are told, the unity in diversity of commodities is designated. The subject of the process is then, as in the first edition, the "immanent contradiction of the commodity," which in the course of a series of "Verdopplungen" generates the determinations of the bourgeois world, including capital and state. Forgotten here is the fact that "commodity" is the form by which private division-of-labor relations stamp the products, and that for historical materialists, insight into the structure-creating dynamic can only result from the reconstruction of human activity within these relations. The "inner contradiction" of the commodity only reflects the antagonism within these relations. The "need to give an external expression to this opposition for the purposes of commercial intercourse," of which Marx speaks, is, by the 'Hegelo-logical' reading, regarded as a popular-didactic, but theoretically misleading, concession. In fact, we still see in the first edition: "This immanent contradiction ... does not rest until it is finally resolved through the doubling [Verdopplung] of the commodity into commodity and money" (MEGA II.5:54). For the second German edition, Marx substitutes the subject "This immanent contradiction" with "das Bedürfnis, diesen Gegensatz für den Verkehr äußerlich darzustellen" (MEW 23:102), and for the French translation with "le besoin même du commerce" (MEGA II.7:66). Marx's thinking had been processed through the interlinguistic 'transformator'. Now it is the "need" of "commercial intercourse," "which finds neither rest nor peace" until the value of the commodity has received its "independent form."

In fact, it appears that Marx had become aware, during his parallel preparations of the Russian and French translations while at the same time preparing the second German edition (see MEGA II.7:715–8), of the danger of a sort of relapse into speculative dialectics. Thus, in the following sentence of the French translation, he substitutes the indeterminate *von Ware* ("of commodity") with the determinate *une marchandise* ("a commodity"): "À mesure donc que s'accomplit la transformation générale des produits du travail en marchandises, s'accomplit aussi la transformation d'une marchandise en argent" (II.7:66).[9] This *one specific* "determinate commodity," gold,[10] is that which underlies the double determination of being at once the use-value gold in the commodity form and the "money commodity" (MEGA II.5:56;

7. Fowkes's translation obfuscates the meaning by putting "the differentiation of commodities into commodities and money" (Marx 1977, 181). It is not "commodities" in general, which is doubled, but the "money commodity." As if he wants to repair the error, he changes the next sentence, too. Where Marx speaks of the *Verwandlung von Ware in Geld* ("the transformation of commodity into money"; MEW 23:102), Fowkes translates, "one particular commodity is transformed into money" (Marx 1977, 181).
8. "This dialectic is modelled on that of Hegel" (Arthur 2002, 160) and it is operating in the "spirit world of capital" (163).
9. For Christopher Arthur's Hegelian reading, it is not this one particular commodity, gold, which "doubles" itself into commodity and money, but the value-form (2002, 31).
10. Marx: "bestimmte Ware"; Fowkes: "single commodity" (Marx 1977, 184).

cf. Marx 1977, 184) par excellence, which embodies the exchange-value of all other commodities.[11]

Why, then, did Marx not adopt for the second German edition the substitution of *von Ware* with the determinate *eine Ware*?[12] We can only speculate. One possibility is that it was so self-evident for him that here he dealt with the "money commodity" and not with commodity as such that the possibility of a Hegelianizing misinterpretation didn't occur to him. Engels, on the other hand, replaces the "doubling of the commodity in commodity and money" with "the differentiation of commodities into commodities and money" (MEGA II.9:75). As if to compensate for the misleading plural, in the following sentence he replaces "the metamorphosis of commodity into money" with "the conversion of one special commodity into money" (76).

A Philosophical Anger

Louis Althusser introduced his 1968 lecture to the Société Française de Philosophie with an anecdote. Lenin, it is said, had declined, laughing heartily, when, during a sojourn in Capri, Maxim Gorki invited him to a philosophical discussion with a group of Bolshevist leftists to which he belonged. This group was convinced that "Marxism had to unburden itself of its pre-critical metaphysics, represented by 'dialectical materialism'"[13] and turned, in the search for an alternative, to the empirio-criticism of the Austrian physicist Ernst Mach. Lenin declined participation in the discussion. "One can then understand Lenin's laughter," Althusser said. "There *is* no philosophical communication, there *is* no philosophical discussion" (Althusser 1969, 10; emphasis added). And, he continued, "Today, I would like to comment just on this laugh, which is in itself already a thesis."

A century later, still under the impression of precritical vulgar metaphysics, into which the Diamat was finally canonized by Stalin, most of us would share the point of departure of the group around Gorki, even if we wished that Lenin had not only laughed but had dealt seriously with the reasons which moved those comrades and had chosen a philosophical path that would have made it impossible for the future state ideology to derive its legitimacy from him. It may be that a philosophical thesis underlay Lenin's laughter, but this thesis could generate a reasonable suspicion that in the name of Marx he fell behind Marx.

Nothing made Marx angrier than when he was confronted with such a reading. Perhaps we may say of Marx's anger, with no less justification than Althusser of Lenin's laughter, that *it is in itself already a thesis*. Although generally justified, this

---

11. In the name of "monetary value theory," which seeks to derive the commodity form from money instead of the money form from commodities, Michael Heinrich has recently argued that the concept of "money commodity" should be eliminated (1999, 233; see my critique in Haug 2004), probably under the impact of the abolition of gold-backing of the currencies. For Marx, it is a key mediating concept to understand modern paper money.

12. The use of the indeterminate article (*une marchandise*) is the form to speak about a determinate commodity (gold).

13. In Althusser's original: "que le marxisme devait se débarasser de cette métaphysique précritique qu'était le 'matérialisme dialectique'" (1969, 9).

anger is occasionally unjust—for example, when Marx snubs a Russian, who cited him, in what we would today call a Eurocentric context, admonishing him to consult the *French* translation, not the *Russian* one. In fact, the former contains, in the chapter that interests us here, extraordinarily important adjustments of emphasis regarding "so-called primitive accumulation," in which a paradigm shift to a no longer monolinear conception of history is expressed. It is on these changes that the undiminished actuality of Marxian theory for the emerging age of transnational high-tech capitalism rests, changes which Engels, contrary to his introductory assurances (see MEW 23:41; Marx 1977, 114), did not adopt in the fourth German edition. Let us look at one of these changes.

Where the fourth edition says of primitive accumulation, "The history of this expropriation assumes different aspects in different countries" (Marx 1977, 876; MEW 23:744), Marx narrows the scope in the French edition to England and Western Europe ("tous les autres pays de l'Europe occidentale") and reduces the claims of the presentation to that of a "sketch" (*esquisse*) (MEGA II.7:634). Hence his reproach of the Russian Marxist Michailovski: "He insists in transforming my historical sketch of the origin of capitalism in Western Europe into a philosophy-of-history kind of theory of the general line of development that fate prescribes for all peoples" (MEW 19:111). Marx's anger signals a leap in consciousness: He is horrified by certain interpretive possibilities of his own main work, *Capital*. His anger includes some unarticulated self-criticism. Yet he can claim to have publicly enunciated it: The French version possesses "a scientific value independent of the original and should be consulted even by readers familiar with the German language" (MEGA II.7:690).[14] What "forced" him "to modify the edition," he says, is in no way due to some inexactitude on the part of Roy. On the contrary, it was precisely Roy's "very scrupulousness" "in producing a version that would be as exact and literal as possible" (Marx 1977, 105).

In this literal exactness, Marx becomes conscious of the fact that his own thinking, to quote *The German Ideology,* "is not 'pure' consciousness": "The 'mind' [Geist] . . . is from the outset afflicted with the curse of being 'burdened' with matter, which here makes its appearance in the form of . . . sounds, in short, of language" (MECW 5:43–4; cf. MEW 3:30). The linguistic materiality of thought, condition and medium of articulated consciousness, is at once its unconscious. Already Hegel, in the preface to the second edition of his *Science of Logic,* observes: "The unconsciousness of this reaches incredibly far." Hegel here shifts the paradigmatic interpretation of his object of knowledge from "the thought of God before the creation," as he said in the preface to the first edition, to the conceptual network of language. It can in no way be said of the intersections of this network, the categories in which forms of thought are regulated, that they "serve us, that we possess them more than they possess us," as long as we have not provided ourselves a certain freedom of movement through reflexion. Marx and Engels take another decisive step here in the direction of the net of vital practices, articulated in historical materiality, a net that maintains a mobile

14. "Welches auch die literarischen Mängel dieser französischen Ausgabe sein mögen, sie besitzt einen wissenschaftlichen Wert unabhängig vom Original und sollte selbst von Lesern herangezogen werden, die der deutschen Sprache mächtig sind" (MEW 23:32).

processual connection with language and thought.[15] They awaken from Hegel's dream of an immobile order of all movement and an abstract predestination of everything concrete.

The overlooking of this concept in the reception of his own work ignited Marx's final anger, which impelled him to undertake, in the *Marginal Notes on Wagner*, a series of further theoretical steps. This final anger, "which is in itself already a philosophical thesis," wells up in him in the face of the bourgeois-academic reading of *Capital* in Germany. Essentially, he takes offense that a conceptual-logical method is attributed to him in which, "through pure reason," the next "phase" is generated from the previous one, as he characterized it when fulminating against Proudhon thirty years earlier. Now he calls it the *Begriffsanknüpfungsmethode*, the method of drawing concepts from concepts, and reproaches the "obscurantist" Wagner with "not even having noticed that my *analytical* method … has nothing to do with the German professorial method of deriving concepts from concepts" (371). Even today Marx is often said to have started with the "concept of the commodity," in which "the concept of money is prefigured" (Altvater 1969, 17),[16] and which is the most abstract category, and so on. In view of an analogous reading, Marx bangs his fist on the table: No, he tells us, he begins with the analysis of the "smallest concrete," the "simplest social form in which the product of labor of contemporary society appears" (MEW 19:369). It would be "scholasticism," he says, to derive exchange-value and use-value from the *value-concept* instead of developing them analytically, starting "from a concretum of the commodity" (*von einem* Konkretum der Ware) (19:362).

When Marx, in *Capital*, examines the opposition between exchange-value and use-value, Rodbertus considers this a "logical opposition" (Marx 1977, 374). In doing so, Marx returns, Rodbertus reads their exposition in *Capital* in logical terms, and the two determinations of the commodity as "pure concepts." If not, he wouldn't have interpreted their opposition as a "logical" one. In reality, Marx continues, in every price list "each individual class of commodity" undergoes "the illogical process" of totally distinguishing itself from the others as a use-value, while "at the same time it presents its *price* as something qualitatively identical but quantitatively different of *the same nature*." "It is a matter here of a '*logical*' opposition only among … [those] who take as their point of departure the 'concept' of commodity, rather than the 'social thing' i.e. the 'commodity', and then make this concept split itself in two [verdoppeln], after which they argue about which of the two phantasms is the real McCoy!" (374 f.). The earlier ambiguity in Marxian language no longer prevails, an ambiguity of which Backhaus correctly says that it leads to "pseudo-theological disputes" (1997, 196). I would add: as long as one refuses, as the same

---

15. On this, see chapter 4 of my *Philosophizing with Brecht and Gramsci*: "'Epistemology must be above all critique of language'—Brecht, Gramsci, and Wittgenstein" (Haug 2006).
16. Similarly, see Lenin (1953– , 38:340), whom my *Vorlesungen zur Einführung ins "Kapital"* [Introductory lectures on "Capital"] (1974/1976, 79 f.) uncritically followed (cf. the completely revised version [2005b, 76 f.]).

Backhaus does, to see Marx's learning process and takes the earlier stage, which is closer to Hegel, as the real thing.[17]

In order to avoid the false dialectic of the value-concept, which appears, through the partial identity of words (use-*value* and exchange-*value*), to point to a contradictory unity of essence, leading to a cosmogonic series of doublings (*Verdopplungen*), Marx maintains a constant linguistic reflexivity in these notes.[18]

In the attempt to grasp the activities of "distinguishing or fixing in the representation" embedded in the net of vital activities, and consequently in language, Marx considers determinations that later are designated by the analytical philosophy of science as "disposition-predicates" ("salt is water-soluble"), yet with categorical reference to human praxis, in which he draws attention to the "for-us" character of these predicates in the sarcastic sentence: "it would hardly occur to a sheep that one of his 'useful' properties is to be edible for humans" (363). He explodes such disposition-predicates by making their anthropocentrism evident.

Here we can certainly no longer say with Althusser that Marx, as he "produced [these concepts] as in a flash of lightning, did not theoretically tie them together and work them out" (Althusser, Balibar, and Establet 1965, 175).[19] No, Marx here is reworking historical-material conditions of validity in the bright daylight of his workshop. These reflections have (in opposition to an understanding of dialectics which often presents itself as a secret art) something liberatory about them. For our rereading today, it is advisable to look for the hints that Marx gives us and bring them to bear retrospectively in the manner of heuristic guidelines. Then one will be on the trail of something of strategic importance: a better understanding of the learning process of the "mature" and eventually "old" Marx. Maybe the main impact of this learning process is a historical materialist rethinking of dialectics.

17. Heinrich objects that in the *Marginal Notes* it is a "not at all a question of Hegelianisms [*Hegeleien*], not even a question of Marx having been accused of such Hegelianism. Rather, Marx criticizes some of the representatives of German vulgar economics" (2004, 94). Here, the decisive aspect is suppressed—namely, that Marx is grappling with the bourgeois reception of Marx, which understands him, according to the paradigm of *Begriffsanknüpfungsmethode*, as merely deriving concepts from other concepts.

18. In doing so, he seeks each time a starting point in reality, in the sense of the first thesis on Feuerbach: in activity, especially the appropriation process out of which the theoretical appropriation arises. Wagner's pseudo-conceptual dialectics recalls the practices of the alchemists, of the "old chemists before the science of chemistry": because cooking-butter is soft, they insist "on the butter character of all chlorides, zinc-chloride, antimony-chloride," and speak of "zinc butter, antimony butter." Or: because "salt" is the first known crystalline and water-soluble material, sugar, for example, is then counted among the "salts" (372). Thus, the philosophical alchemists count use-value as a value. In short, Marx takes cognizance here of similar processes of word stretching on the basis of similar properties, in order to destroy the false conceptual dialectics of "value."

19. "[L]es produisant dans le geste d'un éclair, il n'avait pas rassemblé et affronté théoriquement cette production, ne l'avait pas réfléchie pour l'imposer au champ total de ses analyses" (Althusser, Balibar, and Establet 1969, 175).

Open End

Those who believe in "correcting Marx with Hegel" (as Engels wrote in *Anti-Dühring*) cede this vital terrain to pre-Marxian philosophical ideology. For them, the dialectical point of view is situated at the end of history. Didn't Marx himself declare that "the anatomy of man is the key to the anatomy of the ape"? Yes, he did in the introduction to the *Grundrisse*. But one has to understand that this fragment was never again touched by Marx and, it can be shown, is a failed text.[20] A "rigorously dialectical reading," however, can only be such for historical materialists when it "doesn't read the beginning in the light of that which follows" (Bidet 2004, 60).[21] Indeed, for Marx, "the only materialist, and therefore the only scientific" approach (1977, 494 n. 4) will proceed in the direction of the process and never from what Marx, in volume 2 of *Capital*, calls "the standpoint of the accomplished phenomena" [*fertige Phänomene*] (MEW 24:218; my translation). Against Feuerbach's critique of religion, Marx raises the structurally same objection as against the classical bourgeois economists: "It is, in reality, much easier to discover by analysis the earthly kernel of the misty creations of the religion, than to do the opposite, i.e. to develop from the actual, given relations of life the forms in which these have been apotheosized" (1977, 494 n. 4). Classical political economy has, on the other hand, "analysed value and its magnitude ... and has uncovered the content concealed within these forms. But it has never once asked the question why this content has assumed that particular form, that is to say, why labour is expressed in value" (173 f.). This, however, cannot be developed "from the actual, given relations of life," which are already structured by the value forms. A genetic reconstruction of the transition from more elementary "relations of life" to the actual ones is needed. This is the objective side of what Marxian dialectics is about. The subjective side can be understood as the practical philosophy of Marxism. Here, the approach to a problematic in research has common roots with conjunctural wisdom in social and political struggles as well as in the ancient *techne tou biou*, the art of living, "the greatest of all arts," as Brecht says, whose understanding and practice of a truly new, no longer Hegelian dialectics is one of the most outstanding contributions to an undogmatic renewal of Marxist thought. This understanding of dialectics has not only accepted its limits, but has already incorporated the "aleatory" moment on which, much later, Althusser has insisted. Last but not least, it has inscribed subjective activity in the reality field and, together

---

20. Its formula of "ascending from the abstract to the concrete" as the "scientifically correct method" has its merits, but describes the structure of classical bourgeois science and by no means the specifically Marxian dialectical method as many commentators still believe.

21. Jacques Bidet shares the view that Marx's concept of dialectics is basically Hegelian and that transitions have to be deduced from the 'logical', not practical, "insufficiency of a form, which remained insufficient as long as it was not completely developed" (*tant qu'elle n'était pas complètement déployée*). He concludes: "Therefore it is impossible in this sense to 'pass dialectically' from money to capital" (2004, 101). But when he follows the idea of an "insufficiency" in the sense of not being "completely developed," he does exactly what he rightly condemns—namely, "read the beginning in the light of that which follows." What is more: only in possession of "absolute knowledge" at the "end of history" could one be sure about a phenomenon being "completely developed."

with this, a moment of indeterminacy. Brecht's philosophy of dialectics and dialectics of philosophy, which even among Marxist scholars is still widely unknown, is in many respects congenial to Marx. In a way, Brecht, learning from Karl Korsch, has taken up Marx's learning process. For us who are affiliated with Marx and must learn under pressure of enormous structural ruptures and transformations, plagued by all kinds of political correctness, identity politics, fundamentalisms and sectarianisms, which are as many symptoms of a lack of dialectics, insights into this "work in progress" with a clearer understanding of progress in this work are of vital interest. The task to elaborate a historical materialist understanding of a dialectics without guarantees has perhaps not yet been fully understood, let alone accomplished.

Acknowledgements

This is a revised version of a paper delivered at "Towards a Cosmopolitan Marxism," the Historical Materialism Annual Conference, held 4–6 November 2005 in London. A previous version was presented in German at the conference "Sulle trace di un fantasma. L'opera di Karl Marx tra filologia e filosofia," held 31 March–3 April 2004. This essay was translated by Eric Canepa and reworked by the author. I want to thank my opponent, Chris Arthur, for drawing my attention to some weak spots in the argument and pushing me to rework them.

References

Althusser, L. 1969. *Lénine et la philosophie*. Paris: Maspero.

Althusser, L., É. Balibar, and R. Establet. 1965. *Lire le Capital*, Vol. 2. Paris: Maspero.

Altvater, E. 1969. *Die Weltwährungskrise*. Frankfort: Europäische Verlagsanstalt.

Arthur, C. J. 2002. *The new dialectic and Marx's Capital*. Boston: Brill.

Backhaus, H.-G. 1997. *Dialektik der Wertform. Untersuchungen zur marxschen Ökonomiekritik*. Freiburg: ça ira.

Bidet, J. 2004. *Explication et reconstruction du Capital*. Paris: Presses Universitaires de France.

Haug, W. F. 2003. Wachsende Zweifel an der monetären Werttheorie. *Das Argument* 251 45 (3): 424–37.

——. 2004. Zur Kritik monetaristischer *Kapital*-Lektüre. Heinrichs Einführung in die Kritik der politischen Ökonomie. Parts 1 and 2. *Das Argument* 46 (5): 701–9; 46 (6): 865–76.

——. 2005a. Dialectics. *Historical Materialism: Research in Critical Marxist Theory* 13 (1): 241–56.

——. 2005b. *Vorlesungen zur Einfuhrung ins "Kapital."* New ed. Hamburg: Argument.

——. 2006. *Philosophizing with Brecht and Gramsci*. Historical Materialism Book Series. Boston: Brill.

Heinrich, M. 1999. *Die Wissenschaft vom Wert. Die Marxsche Kritik zwischen wissenschaftlicher Revolution und klassischer Tradition*, 2d ed. Münster: Dampfboot.

Hoff, J. 2004. *Kritik der klassischen politischen Ökonomie. Zur Rezeption der werttheoretischen Ansätze ökonomischer Klassiker durch Karl Marx*. Cologne: PapyRossa.

Kopf, E. 1992. Wann verfasste Marx seine letzte ökonomische Arbeit? In *Beiträge zur Marx-Engels-Forschung, Neue Folge*. Hamburg: Argument.

Kurz, R., ed. 2000. *Marx lesen. Die wichtigsten Texte von Karl Marx für das 21. Jahrhundert*. Frankfort: Eichborn.

Lenin, V. I. 1953–. *Werke*. 40 vols. Berlin: Dietz Verlag.

Marx, K. 1872–5. *Le Capital*. Translated by M. J. Roy, revised by the author. In MEGA II.7.

——. 1887. *Capital: A critical analysis of capitalist production*. Translated from the 3d German edition by S. Moore and E. Aveling, edited by F. Engels. In MEGA II.9.

——. 1964. *Il Capitale. Critica dell'economia politica*. Vol. 1. 5th ed. Translated by D. Cantimori. Introduction by M. Dobb. Rome: Editori Riuniti.

——. 1975. *El Capital. Crítica de la economía política*. 3 vols. Translated by P. Scaron. Mexico City: Siglo XXI.

——. 1977. *Capital*. Vol. 1. Translated by B. Fowkes. New York: Vintage.

——. 1983. *Le Capital. Critique de l'économie politique*. Vol. 1. 4th German ed. Edited by J.-P. Lefebvre. Paris: Messidor/Editions Sociales.

Marx, K., and F. Engels. 1958–. *Werke* [MEW]. 43 vols. Berlin: Dietz Verlag.

——. 1975–89. *Karl Marx-Friedrich Engels Gesamtausgabe* (MEGA). Berlin: Dietz Verlag.

——. 1992–. *Karl Marx-Friedrich Engels Gesamtausgabe* (MEGA). Berlin: Akademie Verlag.

——. 1985–. *Karl Marx/Frederick Engels: Collected works* (MECW). New York: International Publishers.

Plekhanov, G. 1969. *Fundamental problems of Marxism*. New York: International Publishers.

Rehmann, J. 2000. "Abolition" of civil society? Remarks on a widespread misunderstanding in the interpretation of "civil society". *Socialism and Democracy* 1: 1–18.

Reviews

Fragments of Development: Nation, Gender, and the Space of Modernity, by Suzanne Bergeron. Ann Arbor: University of Michigan Press, 2004.

Chizu Sato

What kinds of development become imaginable if we reject 'the national economy' as a legitimate object of experts' understanding and control? Drawing on a combination of antiessentialist Marxian theory, postcolonial theory, and feminist theory, Bergeron examines the mechanisms by which 'the nation' is produced as a manageable economic entity within both mainstream and critical narratives concerned with the question of development. By exposing the multitude of sometimes contradictory knowledges and practices that exist within and outside dominant approaches to the study of development economics, this book resignifies 'the nation' in a manner whose contradictory and heterogeneous effects cascade through and destabilize the interlocking web of signifiers for which it serves as a nodal point. With this text, Bergeron is opening up a space from which we may imagine alternatives that are not visible on terms legitimate within the current apparatus of development.

Key Words: Feminism, Globalization, Development Economics

What kinds of development become imaginable if we reject 'the national economy' as a legitimate object of experts' understanding and control? Bergeron draws on a combination of antiessentialist Marxian, postcolonial, and feminist theory to examine the mechanisms by which 'the nation' is produced as a manageable economic entity within both mainstream and critical development literature. She does so in order to transform the complex of political, cultural, and/or legal structures whose interaction, from their disparate locations on multiple levels, sustains what Inderpal Grewal and Caren Kaplan (1994) have termed "scattered hegemonies." These, for example, provide conditions of existence for exploitative class processes and delimit the field for the legitimate expression of women's capacities while rendering these limits invisible. In the terms of Laclau and Mouffe's discourse theory, *Fragments of Development* would be seen as calling attention to the role of 'the nation' as a *nodal point*, a privileged discursive point, around which discussion of economy, the state, and woman is both structured and is temporarily fixed. By exposing the

ISSN 0893-5696 print/1475-8059 online/06/040585-08
DOI: 10.1080/08935690600901277

Routledge
Taylor & Francis Group

multitude of sometimes contradictory knowledges and practices that are found in and escape representation within dominant approaches to the study of development economics, this book resignifes 'the nation' in a manner whose contradictory and heterogeneous effects cascade through and destabilize the interlocking web of signifiers for which it serves as a nodal point. With this intervention, Bergeron is opening a space from which we may imagine alternatives that are not visible on terms legitimate within the current apparatus of development.

Bergeron begins by exploring how 'the national economy' has, since the end of World War II, been brought into and made central in political debates within development. Chapter 1 offers readers an introduction to processes, such as decolonization movements, socialist planning, and managerial discourses of the economy that emerged from an Enlightenment vision that naturalized the national economy as coherent and as a legitimate object of expert knowledge. Each of the following four chapters focuses on specific aspects of development theory and/or policy. Chapter 2 maps competing strands of growth and modernization theory in the two decades following the end of World War II, examining the dominant Keynesian-inspired strands as well as institutionalist and liberal feminist approaches within the discipline of development economics. It is here that Bergeron explores how Enlightenment notions of knowledge make it possible for experts to conceive of the national economy as a legible and coherent object rather than as a contested site of complex processes. In the Enlightenment tradition, experts who are thought capable of managing 'the national economy' identify what developing nations lack and then prescribe remedies. The national economy is rendered intelligible by the reduction of complex processes to a single set of knowledges in the deployment of what Foucault might call technologies of "simplification." These technologies make it possible, for example, for the state to be seen as a neutral planning authority and for gross national product to be recognized as "the" indicator of growth. Although there were the disruptions of institutionalist and liberal feminist critiques in the late 1960s and early 1970s, these approaches also recognized the national economy as a cohesive and manageable object of analysis. Chapter 3 discusses dependency theory, which emerged in the 1960s and 1970s in Latin America to challenge, among other things, the teleology and stageism assumed by modernization theory. Despite its critical position, this approach was rooted in Eurocentric narratives of capitalocentric development and technology that, like the dominant approaches it sought to challenge, had the effect of marginalizing local ideas and practices. Chapter 4 exposes the analytical underpinnings of the strands of economic thought that inform the structural adjustment programs championed by international development institutions, such as the International Monetary Fund and the World Bank, during the 1980s and 1990s. Bergeron concludes that the analytical under-pinnings of the IMF and World Bank, like those of contemporaneous alternative approaches, constitute economists as value-neutral, detached observers who can produce and deploy the knowledge needed to manage national economies. Chapter 5 looks at debates over "globalization" in relation to development. Bergeron draws on Kayatekin and Ruccio (1998) to argue that mainstream development economists' acceptance of the universality of global capitalism, on the one hand, and their Keynesian-inspired and feminist critics' touting of monolithic interventions by either the state or global social movements to counter global capitalism, on the other, have the common effect of marginalizing diverse ways of recognizing and of organizing economy. Building on Resnick and Wolff (1987), Gibson-Graham (1996), and other progressive feminist development scholars, Bergeron urges the reader to look beyond the naturalized capitalist subject and its narrative of totalizing globalization to discover terms that may enable us to recognize and work from economic difference as a foundation from which we can transform the "scattered hegemonies" of which we are now the unwitting subjects.

Three interrelated aspects of *Fragments of Development* deserve special mention. First, Bergeron offers a critique that challenges the tendency of experts of both mainstream and critical strands of development economics to look outward and blame others for not knowing how to manage "the national economy." Bergeron finds that the problems we currently face are in part an effect of shared assumptions that empower these experts' approaches to the theorization of society. She turns her focus inward, finds, and then critiques the Enlightenment tradition that makes it possible for these experts to imagine themselves to be rational observers independent of the manageable object of their analysis. Second, Bergeron demonstrates a rare ability to call attention to the contradictory and heterogeneous processes at multiple levels and in multiple locations whose simplistic representation is necessary for the emergence of the harmonious, cohesive society that serves as the object of her peers' theorization. By attending to multiple and contradictory processes within both the mainstream and critical strands, this book makes it difficult, if not impossible, to conceive of the nation as a monolithic economic entity. Consequently, Bergeron can critique the leftist experts who are critical of neoclassical approaches yet advocate solutions that require a single actor, be it the state or the global social movement, on the basis that these solutions marginalize local knowledges and exclude other ways of organizing resistances. This move differentiates her from those non-Marxist socialists whose granting to the state the right to appropriate the surplus produced by direct laborers continues the practice of exploitation critiqued by Marx. Finally, Bergeron offers an assessment of and strategies for going beyond the capitalocentrism that characterizes some feminist debates on "globalization." While recognizing the need not to speak in terms of reductive or essentialist representations of women, many feminists uncritically offer their readers an economy and/or a global capitalism that is both monolithic and enormously powerful rather than heterogeneous, contradictory, and potentially vulnerable.

Fragments of Development transforms the capitalocentric dichotomy of the market versus the state and/or the global social movement dichotomy by refusing to accept the Enlightenment tradition fundamental to all parties in this debate. She is interested neither in representing "the reality" nor in offering solutions to existing problems through the deployment of a superior knowledge as, for her, neither is possible. Her interest is to make visible the ideas that underlie development theory, to explore how those ideas are framed, to tease out the effects of this framing on development practice, and, following this through, to study the effects on the women subjects of development found in the global South. A combination of antiessentialist Marxian theory, postcolonial theory, and feminist theory enables her to create new avenues through which it becomes possible to recognize and resist "scattered hegemonies" without succumbing to the temptation to offer yet another simplistic set of solutions. This final point is both the weakness and the strength of the approach Bergeron is taking: we are left without concrete solutions but with the ability to recognize and find interesting the beginnings of paths we could not see previously.

Fragments of Development should be read in light of a few complementary interventions. First, Chakrabarti and Cullenberg's *Transition and Development in India* (2003) enables readers to theorize context-specific, class-based strategies—where class is recognized as processes of production, appropriation, and distribution of surplus. Second, if Foucault's (1997) notion of governmentality is understood as a constantly shifting modality of power that is produced through antagonistic relations between technologies of the domination of others and those of the self, exploration of this modality of power—of how women in the global South not only are shaped but also are shaping development theory and/or policy as agents—would be productive. Finally, Ferguson's (1998) notion of bridge identities and Tamas's (2003) rethinking of experts and their expertise offer readers a means to move beyond monolithic representations of the dominant and its counterpart vanguard politics to explore ways in which we may productively reach out to and form collaborative relationships with the very subjects whose actions sustain the "scattered hegemonies" that are the deserving objects of Bergeron's critique.

References

Chakrabarti, A., and S. Cullenberg. 2003. *Transition and development in India.* New York: Routledge.

Ferguson, A. 1998. Resisting the veil of privilege: Building bridge identities as an ethico-politics of global feminisms. *Hypatia* 13 (3): 95–113.

Foucault, M. 1997. Technologies of the self. In *Ethics: Subjectivity and truth*, ed. P. Rabinow.

Gibson-Graham, J. K. 1996. *The end of capitalism (as we knew it): A feminist critique of political economy.* Cambridge, Mass.: Blackwell.

Grewal, I., and C. Kaplan. 1994. Introduction: Transnational feminist practices and questions of postmodernity. In *Scattered hegemonies: Postmodernity and transnational feminist practices*, ed. I. Grewal and C. Kaplan. Minneapolis: University of Minnesota Press.

Kayatekin, S. A., and D. F. Ruccio. 1998. Global fragments: Subjectivity and class politics in discourses of globalization. *Economy and Society* 27 (1): 74–96.

Resnick, S. A., and R. D. Wolff. 1987. *Knowledge and class: A Marxian critique of political economy.* Chicago: University of Chicago Press.

Tamas, P. A. 2003. Subjects of development: Agency and hegemony within development institutions. Paper read at "Marxism and the World Stage," *Rethinking Marxism*'s 5th International Gala Conference, held at University of Massachusetts Amherst.

Just Around the Corner: The Paradox of the Jobless Recovery, by Stanley Aronowitz. Philadelphia: Temple University Press, 2005.

Richard D. Wolff

Aronowitz shows how U.S. economic development since 1970 has damaged the quantity and quality of jobs with negative consequences for U.S. workers and the economy. An appreciative review nonetheless also urges attention to the social consequences of real wage decline in the United States and the importance of opposition to capitalism beyond struggles between its neoliberal and state-interventionist phases.

Key Words: Jobs, U.S. Workers, Employment

Smoothly written and readily accessible, Stanley Aronowitz's latest book achieves an important current political intervention. He makes three basic points. First, he exposes in detail how U.S. capitalism, especially since the 1970s, has achieved higher profits at the expense of the quality and quantity of jobs for Americans. Second, he nicely contradicts the ideological blizzard that seeks to justify deteriorating jobs; he shows how these are neither a mark of "efficiency" nor a merely temporary problem. The book's subtitle effectively mocks claims that improved quality and quantity of jobs lie "just around the corner."

The book's analytical narrative is couched in a kind of economic history of the United States since the mid-1970s, with special emphases on "the Reagan revolution" and the "Clinton 'boom.'" Central topics include the important role Aronowitz assigns to labor-displacing technological changes and neoliberal globalization. The book concludes with a classic appeal for public policy on job creation, trade, and technological change that rejects reliance on a private sector that has failed to provide good jobs for all.

In style and content, this book argues very well for understanding the last thirty years of U.S. history as a sustained assault on the U.S. working class with profoundly negative consequences for U.S. society as a whole. Students and workers will draw from this book a valuable array of means to better understand and counter Bush's latest steps in the ongoing assault.

Two points might be raised as having deserved more attention than Aronowitz provides. The first concerns the deterioration in U.S. workers' average real wages from 1975 to 2005. For the first time since the beginning of the nineteenth century, U.S. workers suffered decades-long real wage declines. This turnaround in U.S. history is epochal (culturally and politically as well as economically). It has driven more members of working-class families to work more hours at enormous costs to mental and physical health and the quality of human relationships (those failing "family values" that U.S. right-wingers bemoan so religiously even as their leaders' policies destroy them). A working class steeped in a long tradition of rising consumption has also borrowed vast sums to offset falling real wages. Exhaustion, depression, and debt afflict the U.S. working class, adding layers of socially explosive tension and vulnerability to the whole society.

The second point, which Aronowitz acknowledges, also deserves more explicit attention. Neoliberalization (privatization and deregulation at home and abroad) is just the name for one phase of capitalism. The other major phase is state intervention (in its Keynesian and other forms). Capitalism has always oscillated between these forms, each serving as a safety valve for the other. When liberal capitalism hit its worst crisis (e.g., 1929 in the United States, Europe, and beyond), revolution against capitalism was averted by shifting instead to a state-interventionist capitalism. When state-interventionist forms of capitalism encountered their crises (e.g., the 1970s in the United States, Europe, and beyond), the risk of anticapitalist change was deflected onto a shift instead to privatized capitalism. The radical left too often joins battles between oscillating phases of capitalism rather than directing its opposition to capitalism across its phases.

Imaginary States: Studies in Cultural Transnationalism, by Peter Hitchcock. Urbana: University of Illinois Press, 2003.

Maria Markantonatou

In working on the concept of globalization and its impact on culture, Hitchcock is at the same time providing critical arguments on transnational capitalism, on traditional cosmopolitanism theories, and on postmodernism. His elaboration of processes of construction of the national identity and imagination in postnational regimes is based on cultural studies, sociology, and literature. His analysis of Caribbean writers like Glissant examines both the relationship between the local, national, and global culture and the relationship of this global culture to the macroeconomics of global capitalism. The cultural representations of nationhood in globalization, the impact of new processes of capital accumulation on the understanding of (national or local) culture, and the interconnection between the economic, political, aesthetic, and cultural spheres of global capitalism are some of Hitchcock's main theoretical problems.

Key Words: Globalization, Culture, Transnationalism, Postcolonialism, Caribbean Literature

In *Imaginary States*, Peter Hitchcock deals with the concept of "cultural transnationalism" and examines questions of (trans)national identities as well as the representation of nationhood in the frame of global capitalism. His tools of analysis derive from culture studies, sociology, and literature. He focuses especially on the literary works of various Caribbean authors like Glissant, Brathwaite, and Condé. By analyzing their works and the modes of narrativization of the nation-state in the "Caribbean archipelago" —which, according to Hitchcock, embodies four elements: "hybridity, diaspora, postcoloniality and fragmentation" (21) —he is searching for the ways in which literature "exceeds, challenges, demystifies, or transcodes the components of national identity" (9) and reacts not only to political and aesthetic imaginations of the nation-state, but also to new, postcolonial, exploitative forms relating to globalization.

At the same time, Hitchcock discusses critically several cultural aspects and the dynamics of economic globalization in processes of capital accumulation. The "faceless concept of globalization" (188), is, he notes, just as problematic as that of "culture." He understands "globalization" rather as presenting a "nefarious economic system" (186) lacking "a coherent or logical basis for its apprehension" (186). Referring to different works on postcolonial culture (such as those by Fredric Jameson, Arif Dirlik, and Mikhail Bakhtin), he examines the relationship between the "local" and the "global" through the example of Nike in Indonesia. Nike, writes Hitchcock, "is not really in the business of making shoes: What it does is market shoes. The shoes themselves are made through contracting and subcontracting in twelve- to eighteen month production cycles outside its major market, the United States. Currently, Nike uses more than 700 factories worldwide that employ more than 500,000 people (110,000 in Indonesia)" (122). Moreover, inspired by Marx's phrase that "a commodity is a very strange thing, abounding in metaphysical subtleties and theological niceties," Hitchcock studies the rise of a particular commodity-symbol of Western, globalized culture: the commodity defined as "athletic shoes" and the ways through which athletic shoes link culture and capital (119).

One of his most important arguments about culture is related to the historically designated interdependence between economic forms of globalization and culture. Hitchcock considers that the more egalitarian forms of interdependence in globalization cannot be achieved through culture alone, and that, bluntly, "the answer to global capitalism will never be global culturalism" (4). Hitchcock underlines from the beginning that "to pose culture alone as a decisive blow to global modes of economic exploitation is idealist in the extreme (and misleading, since capital can also utilize cultural import/export and culture can exploit sans capital)" (1). On the other hand, he does not adopt the mainstream economist thesis of the primacy of an abstractly defined "global economical system." Despite the apparent validity of terms like "flexible accumulation," "flexi-local production," or "post-Fordist integration of production forged through the free flow of capital around the globe" (187), these terms in Hitchcock's account "only constitute a fraction of economic activity, not just globally but in terms of capital itself" (188) and do not really challenge the "emptiness" (196) of the concept of globalization.

Although "culture" is a central concept in his study of "imagiNation," Hitchcock neither underestimates the role of global capitalism nor overemphasizes mainstream multiculturalist theory, which, according to him, "masks some good old-fashioned hegemonic homogenization" (3). Discussing the traditional cosmopolitanism theory, he criticizes "'We are the world' slogans" (123) and the "Benetton Thesis," reminding us that Benetton, the clothing company, "mixed different clothing colors and races to imply that all are really 'equal' under the law of surplus value" (3).

On "cultural transnationalism," Hitchcock focuses on questions of "transgressive imagiNation" (9): questions of the representation and nonrepresentation of (trans)national culture and of the idea of the Nation in the frame of globalization. Contrary to the poststructuralist view, Hitchcock thinks that the formation of the Nation remains an important instrument of imagination and "a means of normative identification that exerts a tremendous ideological pressure on both political subjecthood and the aesthetics of representation" (4). Whereas the ideas of Nation and nation-state still remain the basic keys of socioeconomic being and reproduction, both to the (intra)individual and at the political level, globality, Hitchcock notes accurately, "arrives as a contaminated and contaminating concept" (7). This "contaminated and contaminating" concept of globality has been projected, he explains, "as a kind of western triumphalism in the apparent absence of significant mass movement alternatives" (7) related to the end of the cold war and the collapse of the Eastern European socialist states. This simplistic starting point explains also, according to Hitchcock, the Endist philosophy of history (7).

Hitchcock's understanding of "cultural transnationalism" as a "critique of Euramerican models of nationhood," which "must continue for many reasons, including that which forestalls any descent into a renewed or reformed colonialism and imperialism" (10), and of the imaginary states as an attempt "to imagine the state otherwise" (10) offer an innovative attempt to avoid reductionism and simplification regarding the "Nation Subject in its Euramerican configuration" (10).

Hitchcock's study of cultural transnationalism can be read in different ways: as a sociology of modern (transnational) culture and its dialectical affinity with (transnational) capitalism, as a philosophical critique of the mainstream paradigms of analysis of cultural globalization, or as a study of literary demystification of national identity through the Caribbean authors he analyzes. The political and aesthetic formation of the Other's identity in globalization reflects on the formation of (transnational) culture, a process that Hitchcock is interested in examining. The abundance of theoretical debates about postmodernism, postcolonialism, globalization, capitalism, and the transnationalization of capital, or about literature and culture studies, are meticulously analyzed, making Hitchcock's book intricate but surely instructive and well articulated. It is enlightening in that problematics, questions, and phenomena related to economic and cultural globalization can no longer be analyzed as separate spheres or in terms of a unilateral discourse, whether concentrating on economic processes of capital accumulation or on aspects of cultural, symbolic order alone. Such issues can be discussed but not exhausted through an interdisciplinary effort, which is what Hitchcock manages to do.

Notes on Contributors

ERIC CANEPA
Previously director of the Socialist Scholars Conference and then of the Left Forum
from 2001 to 2005. He also coordinated the 1998 Manifestivity held at New York's
Cooper Union. He has served as artistic director of Spazio Musica Antica in Florence,
Italy, an early-music concert series. As a harpsichordist and musicologist, he has
performed many concerts and published studies of medieval music. His translations
include the 2005 formal legal complaint (against Donald Rumsfeld and the U.S. chain
of command for torture at Abu Ghraib prison) brought before the German Federal
Prosecutor by the Center for Constitutional Rights.

WOLFGANG FRITZ HAUG
Retired professor of philosophy at Berlin's Free University. In 1959, he founded the
German Marxist journal *Das Argument*, where he remains an editor. In 1980 he
founded the Berlin People's University and also the Berlin Institute of Critical Theory
(InkriT), where he is the scientific director. He is also the editor of the on-going,
multi-volume *Historical-Critical Dictionary of Marxism* (an InkriT project) and
co-editor and co-translator of the complete critical edition of Antonio Gramsci's
Prison Notebooks in German. He has published hundreds of articles and many books.
Among his most well known books are *The Critique of Commodity Aesthetics*;
Commodity Aesthetics, Ideology and Culture; *Elements of a Theory of the
Ideological*; *Philosophizing with Brecht and Gramsci*; *High-Tech Capitalism: Analyses
of Technology, Work, Sexuality, War and Hegemony*; and *Thirteen Essays Toward the
Renewal of Marxist Thought*. Many of these books have been translated and published
in multiple languages.

A. KIARINA KORDELA
Received her Ph.D. at Cornell University and is currently teaching at Macalester
College. Her publications include the articles "Myths of Cultural Studies" (*Cultural
Critique*), "Marx, Condensed and Displaced" (*Interpretation of Dreams/Dreams of
Interpretation*), "Grammar of Secsual and Visceral Reason" (*Parallax*), "The
Democratic Father: Credit and Crime in Metaphor" (*Literary Paternity—Literary
Friendship*), "It Looks Down Upon Us: Allegorical Fields and Repetitive Errors" (*MLS*),
and "Political Metaphysics: God in Global Capitalism" (*Political Theory*).

YAHYA M. MADRA
Teaches economics at Gettysburg College. He has published in the *Journal of
Economic Issues, Rethinking Marxism, Birikim, Toplum ve Bilim*, and *Psychoanalysis,*

ISSN 0893-5696 print/1475-8059 online/06/040593-02
© 2006 Association for Economic and Social Analysis
DOI: 10.1080/08935690600901293

Culture & Society. His research interests include economic methodology, Marxian economic theory, and Lacanian psychoanalysis. He is currently completing his doctoral dissertation, "Late neoclassical economics: The persistence of theoretical humanism in contemporary economic theory," at the University of Massachusetts Amherst.

GEOFF MANN
Teaches in the Dept. of Geography at Simon Fraser University. His research focuses on the political and cultural economy of labor in North America. A book on the cultural politics of the wage in the U.S. West is forthcoming from University of North Carolina Press.

MARIA MARKANTONATOU
Studied sociology and criminology in Panteion University of Athens. Her Ph.D. research at Albert-Ludwigs Universität Freiburg examined the modernization of official social control, focusing on the transformations of the state in the frame of neoliberalism.

CHIZU SATO
Doctoral candidate at the Center for International Education and Women's Studies Program, University of Massachusetts Amherst. She is completing a dissertation on women's empowerment in the international development context.

RICHARD D. WOLFF
Professor of economics at the University of Massachusetts Amherst. With his co-author, Stephen Resnick, he has published many articles and books on Marxist theory and its application to social analysis.